First World War
and Army of Occupation
War Diary
France, Belgium and Germany

55 DIVISION
165 Infantry Brigade
King's (Liverpool Regiment)
7th Battalion
1 January 1916 - 30 April 1919

WO95/2927/1

The Naval & Military Press Ltd
www.nmarchive.com
Published in association with The National Archives

Published by

The Naval & Military Press Ltd

Unit 10 Ridgewood Industrial Park,

Uckfield, East Sussex,

TN22 5QE England

Tel: +44 (0) 1825 749494

www.naval-military-press.com

www.nmarchive.com

This diary has been reprinted in facsimile from the original. Any imperfections are inevitably reproduced and the quality may fall short of modern type and cartographic standards.

© Crown Copyright
Images reproduced by permission of The National Archives, London, England, 2015.

Contents

Document type	Place/Title	Date From	Date To
Heading	1/7th Kings Liverpool		
Heading	1/7 Liverpool Regt Vol XIV		
Heading	1/7th Kings (Lpool) Regt. Jan 1916 Vol XI		
War Diary	Warlus	01/01/1916	06/01/1916
War Diary	Neuville-Au-Bois	07/01/1916	31/01/1916
Heading	1/7 Liverpool Regt. Vol XII February 1916		
War Diary	Neuville-Au-Bois	01/02/1916	04/02/1916
War Diary	Longpre	05/02/1916	05/02/1916
War Diary	St Leger	06/02/1916	06/02/1916
War Diary	Fieffes & Montrelet	07/02/1916	11/02/1916
War Diary	Amplier	12/02/1916	12/02/1916
War Diary	Berles-Au-Bois	13/02/1916	14/02/1916
War Diary	Beaumetz	15/02/1916	15/02/1916
War Diary	Trenches	16/02/1916	29/02/1916
Heading	165th Brigade 55th Division 1/7th Battalion The King's Liverpool Regiment July 1916		
Heading	War Diary Of The 1/7th Liverpool Regt. 165th Infantry Brigade 55th (West Lancashire) Division For The Period 1st July 1916 To 31st July 1916		
Heading	War Diary For The Month Of July 1916 7th Bn. King's (Lpool Regt)		
War Diary	Gouy	01/07/1916	02/07/1916
War Diary	Trenches	03/07/1916	18/07/1916
War Diary	Beaumetz	19/07/1916	19/07/1916
War Diary	Bar Ley	20/07/1916	20/07/1916
War Diary	Gezaincourt	21/07/1916	25/07/1916
War Diary	Mericourt	26/07/1916	28/07/1916
War Diary	Bois-De-Tailles	29/07/1916	31/07/1916
Heading	165th Brigade 55th Division 1/7th Battalion The King's Liverpool Regiment August 1916		
War Diary	Bivouac Near Fricourt	01/08/1916	01/08/1916
War Diary	Caftet Copse	02/08/1916	06/08/1916
War Diary	Support Trenches	07/08/1916	08/08/1916
War Diary	Guillemont	09/08/1916	13/08/1916
War Diary	Caftet Copse	14/08/1916	14/08/1916
War Diary	Ville-Sur Ancre	15/08/1916	19/08/1916
War Diary	Oisemont	20/08/1916	31/08/1916
Miscellaneous	Headquarters, 165th Infantry Brigade	23/08/1916	23/08/1916
Miscellaneous	165 Inf Bde		
Miscellaneous	7th Battalion "The King's" (Liverpool Regiment)	09/08/1916	09/08/1916
Heading	55th Division 165th Infy Bde 1-7th Bn King's L'Pool Regt Jan 1916-Apr 1919 Missing 1917 July & Aug From 2 Div 6 Bde		
Heading	War Diary Of 1/7th King's Liverpool Regt. 1st September To 30th September 1916 Vol 19		
War Diary	Dernancourt	01/09/1916	03/09/1916
War Diary	Trenches	04/09/1916	11/09/1916
War Diary	Buire	12/09/1916	16/09/1916
War Diary	Trenches	17/09/1916	20/09/1916
War Diary	Pommiers Redoubt	21/09/1916	22/09/1916

War Diary	Trenches	23/09/1916	30/09/1916
Heading	War Diary For Month Of September 1916 7 Bn King's (L'pool Regt)		
Heading	War Diary Of 1/7th Liverpool Regt. For The Period 1st To 31st October 1916		
War Diary	Buire	01/10/1916	01/10/1916
War Diary	Buigny-L-Abbe	02/10/1916	02/10/1916
War Diary	Herzeele	03/10/1916	04/10/1916
War Diary	Brandhoek	05/10/1916	05/10/1916
War Diary	Ypres	06/10/1916	10/10/1916
War Diary	Trenches	11/10/1916	15/10/1916
War Diary	C.Camp	16/10/1916	23/10/1916
War Diary	Ypres	24/10/1916	27/10/1916
War Diary	Trenches	28/10/1916	31/10/1916
Heading	War Diary Of 1/7th Liverpool Regt. For Period November 1st To November 30th 1916 Vol 21		
War Diary	Ypres	01/11/1916	03/11/1916
War Diary	Trenches	04/11/1916	07/11/1916
War Diary	C.Camp	08/11/1916	17/11/1916
War Diary	Trenches	18/11/1916	23/11/1916
War Diary	Ypres	24/11/1916	29/11/1916
War Diary	Trenches	30/11/1916	30/11/1916
Heading	War Diary For Month Of November 1916		
Heading	War Diary Of 1/7th Liverpool Regt. For Period December 1st-31st 1916		
War Diary	Trenches	01/12/1916	04/12/1916
War Diary	Ypres	05/12/1916	07/12/1916
War Diary	C.Camp	08/12/1916	17/12/1916
War Diary	Ypres	18/12/1916	22/12/1916
War Diary	Trenches	23/12/1916	27/12/1916
War Diary	Ypres	28/12/1916	31/12/1916
Heading	War Diary Of The 1/7th Liverpool R For The Period 1/1/17 To 31/1/17		
War Diary	Ypres	01/01/1917	02/01/1917
War Diary	Trenches	03/01/1917	07/01/1917
War Diary	B.Camp	08/01/1917	08/01/1917
War Diary	Proven	09/01/1917	09/01/1917
War Diary	Z Camp	30/01/1917	31/01/1917
Heading	1/7 Liverpool Regt Vol XIII March 1916		
War Diary	Wailly	01/04/1916	04/04/1916
War Diary	Trenches	05/04/1916	08/04/1916
War Diary	Beaumetz	09/04/1916	14/04/1916
War Diary	Trenches	15/04/1916	20/04/1916
War Diary	Wailly	21/04/1916	26/04/1916
War Diary	Trenches	27/04/1916	31/04/1916
Heading	War Diary 7th Bn. Kings L'Pool Regt March 1916		
Heading	War Diary Of The 1/7th Liverpool R For The Period 1st To 31st March 1917 Vol 25		
Heading	War Diary For The Month Of March 1917 1/7th Bn The Kings (Lpool Regt.)		
War Diary	Ypres	01/03/1917	03/03/1917
War Diary	Trenches	04/03/1917	07/03/1917
War Diary	B.Camp	08/03/1917	17/03/1917
War Diary	Ypres	18/03/1917	21/03/1917
War Diary	Trenches	22/03/1917	26/03/1917
War Diary	Ypres	27/03/1917	31/03/1917

Type	Location/Description	Start	End
War Diary	Z Camp	01/02/1917	15/02/1917
War Diary	Ypres	16/02/1917	16/02/1917
War Diary	Trenches	17/02/1917	21/02/1917
War Diary	Ypres	22/02/1917	28/02/1917
Heading	War Diary Of 1/7 Liverpool Regt. For The Period 1st To 28th February 1917 Vol 24		
Heading	War Diary Of 1/7th Liverpool R For The Period 1st April To 30th April 1917		
War Diary	Ypres	01/04/1917	01/04/1917
War Diary	Trenches	02/04/1917	07/04/1917
War Diary	B.Camp	08/04/1917	09/04/1917
War Diary	Z. Camp	10/04/1917	16/04/1917
War Diary	Ypres	17/04/1917	17/04/1917
War Diary	Trenches	18/04/1917	23/04/1917
War Diary	Ecole	24/04/1917	29/04/1917
War Diary	Trenches	30/04/1917	30/04/1917
Heading	War Diary Of 1/7th Liverpool R. For The Period May 1st To 31st 1917 Vol 27		
War Diary	Trenches	01/05/1917	01/05/1917
War Diary	R. Sub Sector	02/05/1917	02/05/1917
War Diary	Railway Wood	03/05/1917	05/05/1917
War Diary	B.Camp	06/05/1917	11/05/1917
War Diary	Trenches	12/05/1917	18/05/1917
War Diary	Ypres	12/05/1917	18/05/1917
War Diary	Poperinghe	19/05/1917	19/05/1917
War Diary	Bollezeele	20/05/1917	31/05/1917
Heading	War Diary Of 1/7th Liverpool R. For The Period June 1st To June 30th 1917 Vol 28		
War Diary	Bollezeele	01/06/1917	12/06/1917
War Diary	Mersey Camp	13/06/1917	22/06/1917
War Diary	H.1.A	23/06/1917	23/06/1917
War Diary	Derby Camp	24/06/1917	30/06/1917
Heading	War Diary Of The 1/7 Liverpool R For The Period 1st July To 31st July 1917 Vol 29		
Heading	War Diary For The Month Of July 1917 1/7th Bn The Kings (Lpool Regt.)		
War Diary	Derby Camp	01/07/1917	01/07/1917
War Diary	Westbecourt	02/07/1917	06/07/1917
War Diary	Moringhem	07/07/1917	21/07/1917
War Diary	As detailed for 21st	22/07/1917	25/07/1917
War Diary	Trenches	26/07/1917	31/07/1917
Operation(al) Order(s)	Operation Order No. 93 by Lieut Colonel C.K. Potter Comdg 1/7th Bn "The King's" (L'pool Regiment)	26/07/1917	26/07/1917
Miscellaneous	Appendix 1		
Miscellaneous	1/7th Battalion, "The King's" (Liverpool Regiment)	31/07/1917	31/07/1917
Operation(al) Order(s)	Operation Order No. 93 by Lieut Colonel C.K. Potter Comdg 1/7th Bn "The King's" (Liverpool Regt)	28/07/1917	28/07/1917
Miscellaneous	Appendix 1	31/07/1917	31/07/1917
War Diary	Trenches	01/04/1916	01/04/1916
War Diary	Beaumetz	02/04/1916	07/04/1916
War Diary	Trenches	08/04/1916	13/04/1916
War Diary	Wailly	14/04/1916	19/04/1916
War Diary	Trenches	20/04/1916	25/04/1916
War Diary	Beautmetz	26/04/1917	30/04/1917
Heading	April 1916 War Diary For 7th Bn. Kings L'pool Rg		
War Diary	Wailly	01/05/1916	01/05/1916

War Diary	Trenches	02/05/1916	08/05/1916
War Diary	Wailly	09/05/1916	14/05/1916
War Diary	Trenches	15/05/1916	21/05/1916
Heading	7th Battn "Kings" (Lpool Regt) War Diary For May		
War Diary	Beaumetz	22/05/1916	28/05/1916
War Diary	Trenches	29/05/1916	31/05/1916
War Diary	Trenches	01/06/1916	04/06/1916
War Diary	Wailly	05/06/1916	12/06/1916
War Diary	Trenches	13/06/1916	30/06/1916
Heading	June 1916 War Diary 7th Bn. Kings Liverpool Regt. 55th Division		
Heading	War Diary Of 1/7th Liverpool R For Period 1st To 31st August 1917 Vol 30		
War Diary	Pommern	01/08/1917	03/08/1917
War Diary	Hilloek	04/08/1917	06/08/1917
War Diary	Louches	07/08/1917	31/08/1917
Heading	War Diary Of 1/7 Liverpool R For Period 1/9/17-30/9/17 Vol 31		
War Diary	Louches	01/09/1917	15/09/1917
War Diary	No 2 Area	16/09/1917	17/09/1917
War Diary	Trenches	18/09/1917	23/09/1917
War Diary	Fort Camp	24/09/1917	26/09/1917
War Diary	Barastre	27/09/1917	30/09/1917
Miscellaneous	1/7th Bn. "The King's" (Liverpool Regiment) T.F.	25/09/1917	25/09/1917
Heading	War Diary Of 1/7th Liverpool R For The Period 1st To 31st October 1917 Vol 32		
War Diary	Aizecourt-Le-Bas	01/10/1917	01/10/1917
War Diary	Trenches	02/10/1917	23/10/1917
War Diary	Longavesnes	23/10/1917	31/10/1917
Heading	War Diary Of The 1/7th Liverpool R For The Period 1st To 30th November 1917 Vol 33		
War Diary	Long Aesnes	01/11/1917	02/11/1917
War Diary	Trenches	03/11/1917	16/11/1917
War Diary	Villers Faucon	17/11/1917	17/11/1917
War Diary	Tincourt	18/11/1917	19/11/1917
War Diary	Lempire	20/11/1917	22/11/1917
War Diary	Trenches	23/11/1917	30/11/1917
Heading	War Diary For The Month Of December 1917 1/7th Bn. The Kings (L'pool Regt.) Vol 34		
War Diary	Trenches	01/12/1917	05/12/1917
War Diary	St. Emilie	06/12/1917	06/12/1917
War Diary	Peronne	07/12/1917	08/12/1917
War Diary	Maroeuil	09/12/1917	12/12/1917
War Diary	Tinques	13/12/1917	13/12/1917
War Diary	Brias	14/12/1917	14/12/1917
War Diary	Crepy	15/12/1917	31/12/1917
Heading	War Diary Of 1/7th Liverpool R. For The Period 1st To 31st January 1918 Vol 35		
War Diary	Crepy	01/01/1918	31/01/1918
Heading	War Diary Of The 1/7th Liverpool R For The Period 1st To 28th Febry 1918 Vol 36		
War Diary	Crepy	01/02/1918	08/02/1918
War Diary	Ligny Lez Aire	09/02/1918	09/02/1918
War Diary	L'Ecleme	10/02/1918	12/02/1918
War Diary	Ferme Du Roi	13/02/1918	13/02/1918
War Diary	Windy Corner	14/02/1918	19/02/1918

War Diary	Trenches	20/02/1918	25/02/1918
War Diary	Le Preol	26/02/1918	28/02/1918
Heading	War Diary Of 1/7th Liverpool R For Period 1st To 31st March 1918 Vol 37		
War Diary	Le Preol	01/03/1918	08/03/1918
War Diary	Trenches	08/03/1918	09/03/1918
War Diary	Fme-Du-Roi & Gorr	10/03/1918	14/03/1918
War Diary	Trenches	15/03/1918	27/03/1918
War Diary	Gorre	28/03/1918	30/03/1918
War Diary	Trenches	31/03/1918	31/03/1918
Heading	165th Brigade 55th Division 1/7th Battalion The King's Liverpool Regiment April 1918		
Heading	War Diary Of 1/7 Liverpool R For Period 1st To 30th April 1918 Vol 38		
War Diary	Trenches	01/04/1918	15/04/1918
War Diary	Auchel	23/04/1918	23/04/1918
War Diary	Verquin	24/04/1918	24/04/1918
War Diary	Labourse	27/04/1918	27/04/1918
War Diary	Trenches	29/04/1918	30/04/1918
Miscellaneous	1/7th Battalion, "The King's" (Liverpool Regiment)	17/04/1918	17/04/1918
Heading	War Diary Of 1/7th Liverpool R For Period 1st To 31st May 1918 Vol 39		
War Diary	In The Field	01/05/1918	26/05/1918
Heading	War Diary Of 1/7 Liverpool R For June 1918 Vol 40		
War Diary	Vaudricourt	01/06/1918	02/06/1918
War Diary	Trenches	04/06/1918	14/06/1918
War Diary	Le Preol	15/06/1918	15/06/1918
War Diary	Drouvin Camp	15/06/1918	20/06/1918
War Diary	Trenches	23/06/1918	30/06/1918
Heading	War Diary Of 1/7th Liverpool R For Period 1st To 31st July 1918 Vol 41		
War Diary	In The Field	01/07/1918	31/07/1918
Heading	War Diary Of 1/7th Liverpool R For Period 1st To 31st August 1918 Vol 42		
War Diary	Trenches	01/08/1918	09/08/1918
War Diary	Vaudricourt	10/08/1918	15/08/1918
War Diary	Trenches	16/08/1918	23/08/1918
War Diary	Vaudricourt	24/08/1918	27/08/1918
War Diary	Trenches	30/08/1918	30/08/1918
War Diary	Trenches	01/08/1918	09/08/1918
War Diary	Vaudricourt	10/08/1918	15/08/1918
War Diary	Trenches	16/08/1918	23/08/1918
War Diary	Vaudricourt	24/08/1918	27/08/1918
War Diary	Trenches	30/08/1918	30/08/1918
Heading	War Diary For The Month Of September 1918 1/7th Bn. The Kings (Lpool Regt)		
Heading	War Diary Of 1/7th Liverpool R For Period 1st To 30th Septr 1918 Vol 43		
War Diary	Trenches	01/09/1918	08/09/1918
War Diary	Drouvin Camp	09/09/1918	14/09/1918
War Diary	Trenches	14/09/1918	18/09/1918
War Diary	Outpost Line	20/09/1918	20/09/1918
War Diary	Vaudricourt Camp	21/09/1918	22/09/1918
War Diary	Trenches	23/09/1918	29/09/1918
War Diary	Bethune	30/09/1918	30/09/1918
Miscellaneous	1/7th Bn The Kings (Lpool Regt)	30/09/1918	30/09/1918

Operation(al) Order(s)	Operation Orders No.81 By Lieut. Col. C.K. Potter, D.S.O., M.C. Comdg. 1/7th Bn. "The King's" (L'pool Regiment) T.F.	28/09/1918	28/09/1918
Heading	War Diary For The Month Of October 1918 1/7th Bn. The Kings (L'pool Regt) Vol 44		
War Diary	Bethune	01/10/1918	03/10/1918
War Diary	Le Preol	03/10/1918	05/10/1918
War Diary	Salome	05/10/1918	07/10/1918
War Diary	Hantay	07/10/1918	09/10/1918
War Diary	Grand Moisnil	10/10/1918	10/10/1918
War Diary	La Bassee	10/10/1918	15/10/1918
War Diary	La Bassee Grand Moisnil	16/10/1918	16/10/1918
War Diary	Hocron	17/10/1918	17/10/1918
War Diary	Seclin	17/10/1918	17/10/1918
War Diary	Seclin Fretin	18/10/1918	18/10/1918
War Diary	Fretin Cysoing	19/10/1918	19/10/1918
War Diary	Cysoing Froidmont	20/10/1918	20/10/1918
War Diary	Froidmont Wannehain	21/10/1918	28/10/1918
War Diary	Esplechin	28/10/1918	29/10/1918
War Diary	Froidmont	30/10/1918	31/10/1918
Heading	War Diary Of 1/7th Liverpool R For Period 1st To 30th Novr 1918 Vol 45		
War Diary	W. Of Tournai	01/11/1918	03/11/1918
War Diary	Froidmont	04/11/1918	07/11/1918
War Diary	Fme Du Baron	08/11/1918	08/11/1918
War Diary	Froidmont	09/11/1918	11/11/1918
War Diary	Lanquesaint	12/11/1918	30/11/1918
Heading	War Diary Of 1/7th Liverpool R For Period 1st To 31st December 1918 Vol 46		
War Diary	Lanquesaint	01/12/1918	15/12/1918
War Diary	Enghien	16/12/1918	16/12/1918
War Diary	Buysinghem	17/12/1918	17/12/1918
War Diary	Uccle	18/12/1918	31/12/1918
Heading	War Diary Of 1/7 Liverpool R For Period 1st To 31st January 1919 Vol 47		
War Diary	Uccle	01/01/1919	31/01/1919
Heading	War Diary 1/7th Liverpool R February 1919 Vol 48		
War Diary	Uccle	01/02/1919	09/02/1919
War Diary	Brussels	10/02/1919	18/02/1919
War Diary	Belgium	19/02/1919	28/02/1919
Heading	War Diary 1/7th Liverpool R March 1919 Vol 49		
War Diary	Uccle Brussels	01/03/1919	31/03/1919
Heading	War Diary For The Month Of April 1919 1/7th Bn "The King's" (Lpool Regt.) Vol 50		
War Diary	Uccle Brussels	01/04/1919	30/04/1919

11/7th
Kings Liverpool

1/7 Liverpool Reg^t

Vol XIV

10^c

1/4th King's (L'pool) Regt.
Jan 1916
Vol. XI

Army Form C. 2118

WAR DIARY
or
INTELLIGENCE SUMMARY
(Erase heading not required.)

1st Bn. King's (pool) Regt.

Place	Date	Hour	Summary of Events and Information	Remarks and references to Appendices
WARLUS	Jan'y 1/16	—	Battalion Training, 46 men joined from 3rd line	
"	2nd	—	Sunday. Parades for divine service	
"	3rd	—	Bathing & Coy Parades	
"	4th	—	Coy Drill Parades	
"	5th	—	"	
"	6th	—	"	
NEUVILLE-AU-BOIS	7th	—	Battalion moved to NEUVILLE-AU-BOIS.	
"	8th	—	Company training	
"	9th	—	Sunday. Parade for divine service.	
"	10th	—	Company training	
"	11th	—	"	
"	12th	—	"	
"	13th	—	Inspection by Co.C. 165th Bde.	
"	14th	—	Bathing Parade.	
"	15th	—	Company Training	
"	16th	—	Church Parade. Draft of 50 men arrived	
"	17th	—	Company Training	

WAR DIARY
or
INTELLIGENCE SUMMARY

Army Form C. 2118

2nd SHEET 7th Bn. King's (L'pool) Regt.

Place	Date	Hour	Summary of Events and Information	Remarks and references to Appendices
NEUVILLE AU-BOIS	18.76	—	Company Parades.	
"	19.76	—	" " & Cross country Run.	
"	20.7.	—	" "	
"	21.76	—	Brigade ceremonial Parade.	
"	22nd	—	Company Training & Football.	
"	23rd	—	Church Parade.	
"	24.7	—	Company Training	
"	25.7.	—	" "	
"	26.7.	—	" "	
"	27.7.	—	Battalion Route march.	
"	28.7.	—	Company Training.	
"	29.7.	—	Civil Concentration lunch.	
"	30.7.	—	Church Parade.	
"	31.7.	—	Company Training	

Alfred Miles Major
COMDg 7TH Bn THE KING'S (L'POOL) REGT.

55

1/7 Liverpool Regt.

Vol XII

February 1916

8e

WAR DIARY or INTELLIGENCE SUMMARY

(Erase heading not required.)

Pt. Shek. 7/Bat. King (Liverpool) Regt.

February 1916

Army Form C. 2118

Place	Date	Hour	Summary of Events and Information	Remarks and references to Appendices
NEUVILLE -AU-BOIS	1/2/16	—	Company Parades and firing on Range	
-"-	2nd	—	Coy Parades in the morning. Inspection by Lord Derby in afternoon	
-"-	3rd	—	Coy Parades. Capt. J.J. Ecker to be Temp. Major (¼ L. Gazette dp 29-1-16)	
-"-	4th	—	Coy Parades and shooting competition	
LONGPRE	5th	—	Bn. moved to LONGPRE. 5/5 Bn moving to rest area.	
S.LEGER	6th	—	Bn. moved to ST. LEGER	
FIEFFES	7th	—	Bn. moved to FIEFFES and MONTRELET. Completing move	
MONTRELET	8th	—	Battalion Training	
-"-	9th	—	Battalion Training	
-"-	10th	—	Battalion Training	
-"-	11th	—	Coy and Company officers	
AMPLIER	12th	—	Battalion marched to AMPLIER.	
BERLES-AU-BOIS	13th	—	Battalion marched to BERLES-AU-BOIS.	
-"-	14th	—	Battalion rested.	
BEAUMETZ	15th	—	Bn. moved to BEAUMETZ for the day. In the evening Bn moved to TRENELEY in the MARBOEUF section & took over from the 8/21 French Infantry	

Army Form C. 2118

WAR DIARY or INTELLIGENCE SUMMARY

(Erase heading not required.) 7th Bn. King's (Liverpool) Regt.

Place	Date	Hour	Summary of Events and Information	Remarks and references to Appendices
	Feby 1916			
TRENCHES	Feby 16th		Trenches in very bad state.	
"	17		In trenches nothing unusual in front-line. 3 men wounded accidentally by a party of Bombs exploding.	
"	18		Nothing to report.	
"	19		Enemy lively with Shrapnel. B' moved back to support-line. Carrying and working parties found.	
"	20		do	
"	21		do	
"	22		do	
"	23		B" relieved 9 of King's in Front line.	
"	24		Nothing unusual. Trenches bad. snow fell.	
"	25		— " —	
"	26		— " —	
"	27		Moved back to support-line, relieved by 9 of King's	
"	28		Working & carrying parties found.	
"	29		Working & carrying parties found. Ennever Lieut Colonel	

Comdg 7th Bn King's (L'pool) Regt.—

165th Brigade.

55th Division.

1/7th BATTALION

THE KING'S LIVERPOOL REGIMENT

JULY 1916

War Diary
of the
1/7th Liverpool Regt.,
165th Infantry Brigade,
55th (West Lancashire) Division
for the period
1st July, 1916 to 31st July, 1916.

Secret and Confidential

War Diary.
for.
the Month of
July. 1916.

7th Bn. King's (Lipool Regt)

WAR DIARY
or
INTELLIGENCE SUMMARY

(Erase heading not required.)

Army Form C. 2118

1st Staff — 7th King's (L'pool) Regt.

Instructions regarding War Diaries and Intelligence Summaries are contained in F.S. Regs., Part II. and the Staff Manual respectively. Title Pages will be prepared in manuscript.

Place	Date July/Oct 16	Hour	Summary of Events and Information	Remarks and references to Appendices
GOMMY	1		Drill and instruction.	
"	2		Divine Service parade and relieved East Kents in old system of trenches	
Trenches	3		near Trench Redoubt	
"	4		"	
"	5		"	
"	6		"	
"	7		"	
"	8		GenL Knaggs congratulated the M.O. the very useful information obtained by Patrols of 2/Lt W.G. and E.W. Piper refused trench modern. Brigadier pleased on record the excellent work of the Brigade	
"	9		near Trench Redoubt	
"	10		"	
"	11		"	
"	12		"	
"	13		"	
"	14		"	
"	15		"	
"	16		"	
"	17		"	
"	18		" relieved by 11th Manchesters, moved to fields	
BEAUMETZ	19		BEAUMETZ.	
BARLEY	20		Battalion marched to BARLEY	
GEZAIN-COURT	21		" " GEZAINCOURT.	
"	22		"	
"	23		Divine Service Parade in GEZAINCOURT. Resting and cleaning up.	
"	24		Still under instruction. Transport moved to CARDONNETTE.	
"	25		Battn marched to CANDAS and entrained for MERICOURT entraining about 6 AM 25.7.16	

1875 Wt. W593/826 1,000,000 4/15 J.B.C. & A. A.D.S.S./Forms/C. 2118.

WAR DIARY
or
INTELLIGENCE SUMMARY

(Erase heading not required.) 7th King's (Liverpool) Regt.

Army Form C. 2118

Place	Date	Hour	Summary of Events and Information	Remarks and references to Appendices
MERI-COURT	July 1916 26		Coys under Coy Officers N.9. 1973 Cpl M.S. Bradley & 2577 Cpl M.S. Bradley awarded the Military Medal for Gallant Conduct on the 28 & 29th June 1916 respectively	
---	27		Coys under Coy Officers	
---	28		Bn moved from Mericourt to BOIS-DE-TAILLES. Tents bivouac	
BOIS-DE TAILLES	29		CO 2nd in Comd & Coy Comdrs reconnoitre ground to French Coys in training	
---	30		Bn moved. Bivouac to New FRICOURT. Coy Training	
---	31		Capt. F.H. ROBINSON R.A.M.C attached to the Bn. awarded Distinguished Service Order for gallant conduct on 28/6/16. No. 4937 Pte Currie awarded the Military Medal for gallant conduct on the 28-6-16.	

Fraser
Lieut-Colonel
Comg 7th Kings.

165th Brigade.
55th Division.

1/7th BATTALION

THE KING'S LIVERPOOL REGIMENT

AUGUST 1916

Army Form C. 2118

WAR DIARY
or
INTELLIGENCE SUMMARY
(Erase heading not required.) 7. KINGS. (LPOOL) REGT.

Instructions regarding War Diaries and Intelligence Summaries are contained in F.S. Regs., Part II. and the Staff Manual respectively. Title Pages will be prepared in manuscript.

SHEET I

Place	Date August	Hour	Summary of Events and Information	Remarks and references to Appendices
BIVOUAC NEAR FRICOURT	1		Move Bivouac to near CAFTET COPSE	
CAFTET COPSE	2		Coys at Training	
"	3		" " "	
"	4		" " "	
"	5		" " "	
"	6		Church Parade. Moved up to support 5th Kings.	
Support Trenches	7		In support Trenches near TRONES BOIS. Working Parties	
"	8		Moved at 11 pm to relieve 5th Kings.	
GUILLEMONT	9		Small attack on German Trenches. Captn. O. MOTTRAM, 2/Lt. E.R. THOMAS and 2/Lt. MATTHEWS killed. Lieut. T.H. LYON, R.F. MARKEY, E.S. TAYLOR & Capt. W. Porter wounded.	
"	10		Trenches heavy cannonade.	
"	11		Capt. A.H. Robinson wounded. Attached to Burmah not engaged. Trenches	
"	12		Trenches. Nearer Reconnaissance continued.	
"	13		August D 12th Y/Z/3 7 Ly 1/Kings 15. Coy's at to relieve Battalion. 1 Coy J.C.K. King's and 2 Coys 15 J. Kings attempted to capture German trench but not successful. During the next 5 days the following casualties were sustained. Other ranks 36 killed 113 wounded, 10 missing. 5 Officers killed T.H. FEARNHEAD & E.W. PORTER wounded. Battalion in Reserve Nr CAFTET COPSE.	
CAFTET COPSE nr VILLE-SUR ANCRE	14		Bn. moved to VILLE—SUR.ANCRE	
"	15		Bn. in billets. Inspection by G.O.C. 55th Divn.	
"	16		" " Coy Training & Bathing.	
"	17		" " " "	
"	18		Transport moved by march route at 3.30 pm Draft of 166 Manchesters joined.	

Army Form C. 2118

WAR DIARY
or
INTELLIGENCE SUMMARY

(Erase heading not required.) 7th K'ing's (Liverpool) Regt

2 SHEET

Instructions regarding War Diaries and Intelligence Summaries are contained in F.S. Regs, Part II. and the Staff Manual respectively. Title Pages will be prepared in manuscript.

Place	Date Aug/16	Hour	Summary of Events and Information	Remarks and references to Appendices
VILLE-SUR-ANIRE	19		B'n marched to MERICOURT at 3 A.m. entrained and reached PONT REMY at about 10.30 a.m. detrained and marched to OISEMONT. Lieut E.S. Taylor died of wounds.	
OISEMONT	20		Church Parades 2/Lt E.W. BATER died of wounds.	
"	21		Coy Training	
"	22		" "	
"	23		" "	
"	24		" " Draft- 965 men 9/9 men & other joined Battalion	
"	25		" "	
"	26		Church Parades	
"	27		Battalion Training 32 men 7th K'ings joined from 9th K'ings.	
"	28		" " 20 " 2/9 Manchester joined Battalion	
"	29		Battalion marched from Oisemont at 1 p.m. to PONT REMY and entrained for MERICOURT	
"	30		Detrained at MERICOURT at 5.30 a.m. & marched to Bivouac Area near DERNANCOURT. Battalion moved at 2.30 p.m. from Bivouac Area to Billets performed in DERNANCOURT.	
"	31			

R.A. Bridges
Capt.
Capt & K'ings

1875 Wt. W593/826 1,000,000 4/15 J.B.C. & A. A.D.S.S./Forms/C. 2118.

To Headquarters,
165th Infantry Brigade.

On the night of the 8th August the Battalion received orders to go into the trenches and be prepared to attack at dawn. These orders were explained to Company Officers and their frontages given to them prior to going into the trenches. Guides led the Companies up to their positions.

"A" Company, owing to the uncertainty of the guides, and the fact that the trench they were supposed to "jump off" from did not exist, as shewn on the map, found themselves at "Zero" in the open, without any idea of where their objective was, and dug themselves in in a shallow half-dug trench about 100 yards to the left rear of SHUTE'S TRENCH, and as it afterwards turned out, almost opposite their objective. "B" Company, misled by their guides, got to their position just at "Zero"; which position had to be reached over the open. They were completely out of touch with the right attacking Company ("A"). They were seen by the enemy and suffered some casualties getting there. "C" Company and Bombers attempted to attain their objective but owing to a lack of accurate knowledge of the ground and the position of the enemy were repulsed. "D" Company were in Reserve.

During the morning of the 9th we obtained touch with all Companies but "B", who were in a strong position in front with no Communication Trench back. During the day all positions were consolidated.

On the night of the 9th "A" Company, commenced to join up to SHUTE'S TRENCH. "B" Company sent out a party for water, but this party, owing to the loss of direction, failed to get back to their Company. An attempt was made to relieve a Machine Gun which was in the vicinity of "B" as the Gun was without water and ammunition. This also failed for the same reason. During the night our "Barrier" was heavily shelled and for a short period the best part of the Garrison were withdrawn into adjoining trenches until the shelling finished when they returned to the "Barrier" and commenced repairing the damage done.

On the morning of the 10th Captain Owens ("FRED") and the Machine Gun were relieved.

On the night of the 10th a Company and a half of the Pioneer Battalion, under R.E. supervision, dug a trench from a point South of our "Barrier", via the Strong Point, towards "B" Company (OWEN'S TRENCH). This work was completed by the night of the 12th.

On the same night (10th/11th) "A" Company, assisted by half a Company of Pioneers, dug a Trench across to "B" Company, which was completed on the following night; and also completed the connection of their line with "C" Company of "WILLIE" (SHUTE'S TRENCH).

On the same night "B" Company were revictualled but received no water until the following night.

On the night of the 11th an attack was made by "D" Company and the Bombers on the German "Barrier", which they reached but had to retire as it was very strongly held by the enemy.

"A" Company (ASSEMBLY TRENCH) during the same night joined up the Southern flank of OWEN'S TRENCH with the new Communication Trench.

On the night of the 12th a determined effort was made to dig the direct trench from the "Barrier" to the Northern flank of OWENS TRENCH. Preparations were made during the day to ensure the right direction being maintained - a wire was run across and as a further precaution a compass bearing was given and green flares sent up. This work was duly completed. Instructions were also received to join up the Southern flank of OWEN'S TRENCH and the Northern flank of SHUTE'S TRENCH with the new trench lying to the East of our positions (DOUBTFUL TRENCH). As this trench was held by the enemy it was of course necessary to drive them out first. A Company of "WILLIE" and two Companies of "WALTER" were detailed for this task and great difficulty was experienced getting them into position in the ASSEMBLY TRENCH in time owing to the lack of guides who at the time were conducting the relieving Companies into their positions. This attack was arranged as a surprise there being no Artillery preparation, but was detected when half was across and repulsed with loss by heavy Machine Gun fire, by which time dawn prevented a further attempt without arrangements with the Artillery.

Our relief was carried out by mid-day on the 13th instant.

Captain,
Commanding 7th Battalion "The King's" (L'pool Regt.)

23rd August 1916

"A" Form.
MESSAGES AND SIGNALS.

TO: 165 Inf Bde

Sender's Number: N63
Day of Month: 16

Reference to your G 384/1 I append copies of Daily Situation Reports which is roughly a précis of what happened.

Ruearick
Lt Col
Comdg

From: 4 B Kings

7th Battalion "The King's" (Liverpool Regiment).

SITUATION AT 12 NOON 9. 8. 1916.

At "Zero" the situation was as follows :- (4.30 a.m 9/8/16)

The left front Company was in position. The right Front Company was in Line but too far South. The Third Line Company was in position. The Fourth Line Company (One Company "WILLIE") was in position and the fifth Company was in Reserve. All these Companies came into action with the exception of the Front Right Company. The O/C (Capt. Thompson) recognising that he was too far South did not advance. Heavy Machine Gun fire was at once encountered, mainly from the Barrier, and from the end of COCHRANE TRENCH. This stopped the advance, although the enemy were not hand-to-hand. The Bombers attacked their objective but were repulsed *losing their Officer. I then ordered Capt. Thompson, O/C Right Company, to advance towards his point of deployment and immediately organise the Battalion with a view to being in position to carry on the attack when ordered. The "Stokes" Section were issued with further ammunition. In the meantime I had sent one Platoon from the Reserve Company to help the Bombers, but they were unable to make progress. In my opinion the C.T. which marks our left flank is more strongly held than anticipated. The difficulties of getting into position for deployment were accentuated by the Guides who, through no fault of "FRED" did not know, and could not be made to understand the location required, and there are no landmarks to work on. The Battalion is now digging a continuous trench on the frontage occupied and this will be held to-night by three Companies (less 1 Platoon) in the Front Line, roughly estimated at 1,200 yards, with their Lewis Guns and 5 Machine Guns. The one Platoon will be on our extreme left where SUNKEN ROAD bends back. One Company in EDWARDS TRENCH in Support, with its Lewis Guns and three M.G's. No. 2 Battalion (WILLIE), with one Company in Reserve in SWAINSON TRENCH, and three Companies in DUBLIN and CASEMENT TRENCHES. The remaining 8 M.G'S in Reserve under the M.G. Officer.

*Lt-Bosh afterwards arrived with B. Coy.

SITUATION AT 2 A.M. 10. 8. 1916.

"A" Company is consolidating (on line shown). I await report from right Company ("C" - "WILLIE"). "B" Company has been located and is working towards "A". "C" Company is rather indefinate. M.G. in strong Point is being revictualed, men and ammunition were exhausted. Pioneers were distributed, 50 to "C" Company and 50 to "A" Company. *Barrier was blown in completely and we are consolidating about 50 yards further back. The O/C at this point reports - "Position secure at 11-30 p.m." The Artillery (British) has caused us casualties and I suggest the German barrier be carefully registered by an F.O.O. and systematically dealt with. It is a strong point. The C.T. from here to T.C.4.8. is very strongly held and our M.G. in strong point is rather exposed but necessary. Our arrangemnets for consolidating were going on smoothly until the shelling commenced. It was heavy and disorganised arrangements.. Capt. Owens ("FRED") has been relieved and reports "BROCK" in charge of "B" Company vice "PATON" and digging well. The position of this Company "B" is rather advanced. Both "B" and "A" Companies are digging towards each other and their junction is an urgent matter for "B" who have been isolated all day. We got water to them last night.

*Barrier was retaken at dawn.

SITUATION AT 12-30 A.M. 11. 8. 1916.

"A" Company slightly to the rear of "WILLIE'S" Company, has joined up with its left flank, and from this trench is working towards "B" Company. The latter, by arrangement is letting off Flares in order that the exact location may be obtained both for "A" Company (with 50 South Lancs) and the party of 185 men (S. Lancs.) working from vicinity of rear of Barrier. "C" Company are on the left and overlap the Barrier. This company has lost rather heavily in repairing and retaining this position from which they were first driven from. "D" Company is in Reserve and WILLIE'S Company hold our right flank. On both flanks we are in touch with the next troops. Trench Name Boards have been made and are ready to be fixed. The result of operations on night of 8th/9th left rather a weak gap in our left flank, so the 50 men (4th S. Lancs) with M.G's were placed in trench at junction of SWAINSON and JACKSON TRENCHES facing N.E. Two Platoons of Reserve Company were sent ot Barrier to consolidate and one of these has been withdrawn to the Reserve. The chief work to-night is the construction of a continuous trench from Barrier to "B" Company and "B" Coy to "A". This will not be an easy task as the enemy have opened a continuous rifle fire.

SITUATION AT 2-45 A.M. 12.8.1916.

As a result of last night's work we considerably relieved "B" Company's position and completed a continuous line of trench, though in some places very shallow, round the whole of our position. Owing to the Local difficulties the alignment is not good. A total length of nearly 1,000 yards has been dug. During the night a Bombing attack on our isolated "B" Company was repulsed and one prisoner captured, who has since died of wounds. Some of the trenches encountered on our front are full of German dead. The German captured was of fine physique and very well equipped, evidently a Jaegar. The feature of to-day has been the systematic shelling of our trenches by our own Artillery, both heavy and light and we have lost many good men through this. Complete Liason is established with the French and our two H.Q. are now connected by Phone. The French are carrying out minor operations on our right to-night. From experience it is quite evident that the Valley in which our H.Q. are situated is included in the German Barrage, as it is heavily shelled on every outburst of "Liveliness". To-night at 10-30 we attempted to take the German Barrier at S.30.b.65.15. by a sudden rush of Bombers followed by a consolidating party - a total of 44 men and two officers, with 20 men to dig in. they were immediately received with heavy Rifle Grenade, Rifle Fire and Bombing. The Germans then manned the Barricade and with loud shouting opened fire. An officer's estimate of the number here was 30 or more, and the trench to the right was also strongly held. Our four men reached their right flank but were driven back and then red and green lights went up in numbers, and an extremely heavy barrage opened on our lines. This was the heaviest we have known and disorganised our wires and destroyed the wireless. The Germans hold this Barrier very strongly and are absolutely alert. The various plans to-day have necessitated some readjustment of my line and I append location and distribution of the troops at present under my command. It appears to me that the line could be held by three strong companies and two in support, but mine are weak.

SITUATION 12. 8. 1916.

      The day has been spent in consolidation. The arrival of a new aeroplane photograph confirmed our suspicions as to the presence of Germans nearer to us than their Road Line. Later on instructions were received to attack and consolidate this trench. Owing to a relief being in progress the organisation of this was a difficult question. ultimately two Companies from other Battalions were placed at our disposal and at 4-35 we advanced. The attack was unsuccessful as the trench was strongly held by M.G's. Our relief was carried on and by mid-day of the 13th was complete.

Lieut-Colonel,

Commanding 7th Battalion "The King's" (Liverpool Regiment).

17th August, 1916.

55TH DIVISION
165TH INFY BDE

1-7TH BN KING'S L'POOL REGT
JAN 1916-APR 1919

(MISSING 1917 JULY & AUG) (NO)

FROM 2 DIV BDE

55TH DIVISION
165TH INFY BDE

165/55

No 19

15.e

War Diary

of

1/7th King's Liverpool Regt.

1st September to 30th September 1916

Army Form C. 2118.

WAR DIARY
or
INTELLIGENCE SUMMARY

(Erase heading not required.)

SHEET I   7th Kings (L'pool) Regt

Instructions regarding War Diaries and Intelligence Summaries are contained in F.S. Regs., Part II. and the Staff Manual respectively. Title Pages will be prepared in manuscript.

Place	Date Sept/16	Hour	Summary of Events and Information	Remarks and references to Appendices
DERNANCOURT	1st		Company Training and Inspections	
-do-	2nd		Company Training and Construction of Strong Point - Capt. Rutherford. Wounded	
-do-	3rd		Church Parades. Recently joined drafts inspected by Brigadier at 9 a.m. Construction of Strong Point.	
Trenches	4th	4.15	Battalion moved from DERNANCOURT to Trenches between DELVILLE WOOD & HIGH WOOD. Relieved Bn Northampton Regt.	
do	5th	5.15	Relief completed by 5 a.m. C & D Front line. A & B Support. 2nd Lt. Rhodes wounded	
do	6th		Bombing attack on TEA TRENCH. 2/Lt B. Cook, missing. 2/Lt Bell & Yeoman wounded. Captain Randall R.A.M.C. wounded.	
do	7th	7.15	Battn moved into support of 9th Kings	
do	8th	8.15	Working parties & salvage.	
do	9th	9.15	Battn moved into front-line (2 coys 'B' + 'C') 2/Lt Harrison. H. wounded.	
do	10th	10.15	'A' and 'D' coys (in support) relieved by 2nd N.Z. R.B.	
do	11th	11.15	'B' and 'C' coys (in front line) relieved by 11th Queens.	
BUIRE	12th	12.15	Battn moved to BUIRE-SOUS-CORBIE. During last 9 days, casualties - 9 killed, 83 wounded, 5 missing, 2 died of wounds Inspections and Coy Training	

Army Form C. 2118.

WAR DIARY
or
INTELLIGENCE SUMMARY

7/15 Kings Liverpool Regt

SHEET 11

Place	Date	Hour	Summary of Events and Information	Remarks and references to Appendices
BURE	13		Company Training. 21 Men joined Battn. Bathing	
-do-	14		Company Training. Bathing. Lecture by Brigadier to all Officers & N.C.Os	
-do-	15		Battn Training in Attack	
-do-	16		Battn moved into Bivouacs at DERNANCOURT	
Trenches	17		Battn moved into Trenches at FLERS. Relieved a Battn of the 64th Infy. Bde. Continuous rain for 24 hours. Line of S.P. commenced & continued.	
	18		Battn relieved in front line moved into Carlton & Savoy Trenches	
	19		Draft of 17 Men joined Battn. Carlton & Savoy Trenches.	
	20		Battn relieved in support by 8/15 K.L.R. and moved into Bivouacs at POMMIERS REDOUBT. Casualties in last four days 2 Killed, 16 Wounded 16 Missing.	
POMMIERS REDOUBT	21		Coys Cleaning up and Inspections, refitting etc.	
	22		Coy Training	

WAR DIARY
or
INTELLIGENCE SUMMARY

Army Form C. 2118

Sheet III

Place	Date	Hour	Summary of Events and Information	Remarks and references to Appendices
Trenches	Aug 23 24	night	Battn relieved 5th Battn L.N.Lancs, in front line FLERS, C&D front line A&B Support line, relief complete 1-0am	
	24		Improving Trenches, patrolling & preparing to attack 2/Lt Chalmers A.L. killed.	
	25		Attacked & gained possession of – GOAT & GIRD TRENCH, GIRD SUPPORT, SUNKEN ROAD – GUEUDECOURT – FACTORY CORNER. Reinforced by 1 Coy 5th K.L.R in SUNKEN Rd at 11-15 p.m. + 8th K.L R in GIRD TRENCH at 1.2am 26/9/16. – 2/Lt LEWIS, PATTERSON, TURNBULL, killed in action. 2/Lt LACE P.W. H+B Actg TOONE, Lt-Col. POTTER CK, Lt. NESBITT R.D, 2/Lts BELL S.J., TANNER, ROBERTS HAISALL A.R. LT CRUICKSHANK J.N. (RAMC) Wounded in action. Capt Ropers L.H., 2/Lt RAWCLIFFE WOUNDED Shell Shock.	
	26.		Consolidating Trenches. Relieved by 4th L.N.Lancs in GIRD TR. & by 8th K.L.R in Sunken Road. Relief complete 1-45 am (26/27.) Moved into Carlton & Savoy Trenches	
	27		CARLTON & SAVOY TRENCHES. Casualties in past five days, 43 killed 197 Wounded, 3 Shell Shock, 21 missing	
	28		Moved into Billets at BUIRE.	
	29 30		Coy Inspections & Training	

E.M.Brandes Major
Commdg 7th K.L.R

SECRET AND CONFIDENTIAL

WAR DIARY
FOR
MONTH OF SEPTEMBER
1916

1/BN KING'S (L'POOL REGT)

CONFIDENTIAL

Vol 20

52 / 16ᵉ

War Diary
of
1/7th Liverpool Regt.
for the period
1st to 31st October 1916

Army Form C. 2118.

WAR DIARY
or
INTELLIGENCE SUMMARY

(Erase heading not required.)

1st SHEET 7 Kings (L'Pool) Regt

Instructions regarding War Diaries and Intelligence Summaries are contained in F.S. Regs., Part II. and the Staff Manual respectively. Title Pages will be prepared in manuscript.

Place	Date	Hour	Summary of Events and Information	Remarks and references to Appendices
DOIRIE	Apl/16 1st			59A
BUSANY-L-ABBI	2nd		Moved to BUSANY-L-ABBI via LONGPRE by Rail and Road	
HERZEELE	3rd		" HERZEELE by Rail and Road	
"	4th		Rested the day	
RENINGHOEST	5th		Moved to BRANDHOEK by Rail and Road	
YPRES S.	6th		Relieved the 9 Kings in support at YPRES S.	
"	7th		in support	
"	8th		"	
"	9th		"	
"	10th		Relieved 9 K Kings in front line	
TRENCHES	11th		Went to front line	
"	12th		"	
"	13th		"	
"	14th		Relieved by 8th Kings (L'pool Regt) and moved by Tram Road to "C" Camp	
C.Camp	15th		Cleaning up and Inspection	
"	16th		Coy Training	
"	17th		Othr ranks Trench digging	
"	18th		Coy Training	
"	19th		Coy Training	
"	20th		Working Parties. This morning Inspection by Corps Comdt	
"	21st		Trench Mortar Brigade presented Medals to those who were recommended them for services on the Offensive.	

2449 Wt. W14957/M90 750,000 1/16 J.B.C. & A. Forms/C.2118/12.

Army Form C. 2118.

WAR DIARY
or
INTELLIGENCE SUMMARY

(Erase heading not required) KINGS (LPOOL) REGT

Instructions regarding War Diaries and Intelligence Summaries are contained in F. S. Regs., Part II. and the Staff Manual respectively. Title Pages will be prepared in manuscript.

Place	Date	Hour	Summary of Events and Information	Remarks and references to Appendices
C. Camp	23		Inspection by 8th Corps Commd. Marched to BRANDHOEK restcamp	
YPRES	24		Coy Training etc	
"	25		WORKING PARTIES	
"	26		Drill, Inspections and working parties	
"	27		Relieved 9th Kings in front line.	
TRENCHES	28		Usual Trench Routine	
"	29		"	
"	30		"	
"	31		Relieved by 9th KINGS and returned to YPRES in support	

54
30

M Grandes Major
Comdg 4th Kings (L'pool) Regt

CONFIDENTIAL

Vol 21

War Diary
of
1/7th Liverpool Regt.
for period
November 1st To November 30th 1916

17c

WAR DIARY or INTELLIGENCE SUMMARY

Army Form C. 2118.

1/5 J.HEET 1/7 Bn KING'S (LPOOL) REGT

Place	Date Nov 1915	Hour	Summary of Events and Information	Remarks and references to Appendices
YPRES.	1		In support. Working parties found.	
"	2		"	
"	3		"	
TRENCHES	4		Relieved 9.K.King's in "Front" Trenches. Trench duties, nothing unusual.	
"	5		"	
"	6		"	
"	7		Lt-Col. C.K.POTTER rejoined.	
C. Camp.	8		Relieved by 1/8.King's 1/pool Regt, and moved by Rail and Road to C Camp.	
"	9		Inspection and Coy Training.	
"	10		Baths. Coys under Coy Officers.	
"	11		Inspection of Coy specialists by CO.	
"	12		Voluntary Church Parade. Coys Company Drill from.	
"	13		Coys under Coy Officers and CO. Rifle inspection & musketry.	
"	14		Ceremonial Battalion Parade. Presentation of medals by Gen Officer Comdg. Corps. Officers and CO. Parade.	
"	15		" Parade attack with 1 Bn 9.Manchesters.	
"	16		"	
TRENCHES	17		Two Bns practice alarm.	
"	18		Inspection. Railed to YPRES and took over Billets from 1/8.King's.	
"	19		Relieved 2/5.LANCS.Fus. in Left sub sector Right. Sec.	
"	20		Trench duties, nothing unusual.	
"	21		"	
"	22		"	
"	23		" Relieved by 9.K.King's & moved to YPRES.	

WAR DIARY
or
INTELLIGENCE SUMMARY

(Erase heading not required.) 7 KING'S L'POOL REGT.

2nd SHEET.

Army. Form C. 2118.

Place	Date	Hour	Summary of Events and Information	Remarks and references to Appendices
YPRES	24-1-16		Working Parties and Coy Parades.	
"	25		" " " "	
"	26		" " " "	
"	27		" " " "	
"	28		" " " "	
"	29		" " " Relieved the 9th KING'S —	
TRENCHES	30		the front line Trenches	

2nd Dec! 1916.

C.B. Stru. Lt. Colonel.
Comdg 7 th Kings (L'pool) Regt.

1/15 Kings (L'pool Regt)

WAR DIARY

FOR

MONTH OF

NOVEMBER 1916

SECRET

CONFIDENTIAL

Vol 22

18e.

War Diary

of

1/7th Liverpool Regt.

for period

December 1st – 31st 1916

WAR DIARY or INTELLIGENCE SUMMARY

Army Form C. 2118.

Sheet 1. of MANNING'S (POOL) REGT.

Place	Date	Hour	Summary of Events and Information	Remarks and references to Appendices
TRENCHES	Oct 1/16		Usual Trench Routine	
"	2		"	
"	3		"	
"	4		"	
"	5		relieved by 9th Kings – Trench R't & YPRES 2/Lt H.H. WEYMAN attached.	
YPRES	6		Cleaning up and working parties. Ptes BROOKFIELD & HOWARD awarded	
"	7		Working parties. Lt/Col OSBORN Bn moved to C Camp by Rail YPRES	
C.Camp	8		Initially training.	
"	9		Company Training	
"	10		Church Parade and working party	
"	11		Company Training	
"	12		"	
"	13		"	
"	14		"	
"	15		Church Parade & working party.	
"	16		Bn. moved to YPRES by Rail & foot.	
YPRES	17		Coy Training and working parties. 2/Lt P.N. LAGE evacuated	
"	18		Working Coys	
"	19		Coy training and working parties.	
"	20		"	P.T.O.

Army Form C. 2118.

WAR DIARY
or
INTELLIGENCE SUMMARY

(Erase heading not required.) 1/KINGS (Lpool) REGT.

2 NO SHEET

Instructions regarding War Diaries and Intelligence Summaries are contained in F. S. Regs., Part II. and the Staff Manual respectively. Title Pages will be prepared in manuscript.

Place	Date April 16	Hour	Summary of Events and Information	Remarks and references to Appendices
YPRES	21		Coy Training yesterday practice	
"	22		Relieved 9/K Kings in the Trenches	
TRENCHES	23		Front line Trenches badly knocked about.	
"	24		Heavy Trench Mortars	
"	25		" "	
"	26		" "	
"	27		relieved by 9/K Kings	
YPRES	28		" "	
"	29		Coy Training and working parties	
"	30		" "	
"	31		" "	

J.M. Potter

C.W. Potter Lt Colonel
Comdg 1/the King's (Lpool) Regt

Vol 23

19e.

War Diary
of the
1/7" Liverpool R
for the period
1/1/17 to 31/1/17

WAR DIARY
or
INTELLIGENCE SUMMARY

Army Form C. 2118.

(Erase heading not required.) 4th KING'S (LPOOL) REGT

1st Week

Place	Date	Hour	Summary of Events and Information	Remarks and references to Appendices
YPRES.	July 1.		No parades or Working parties. Free Burial. Battalion dined together in the Church.	
"	2.		Working parties in the morning. Relieved 9th King's in Trenches at night.	
TRENCHES	3.		Usual Trench Routine.	
"	4.		"	
"	5.		"	
"	6.		"	
"	7.		Relieved by 9/S Lanc Fus. and proceeded to B. Camp	
B. Camp.	8.		B" march to PROVEN. 2nd O.C.Parade of Bn. left behind in B.Camp	
PROVEN.	9.		Ceremony and Inspection. 2 other Coys & D Coy to Detachment - BEEGWES.	
"	10.		Battalion detailed for Railway construction work overseas Coy R.E.s	
"	11.		"	
"	12.		Battalion bathed at Chateau COUTHOVE.	
"	13.		Railway construction work. Major Harris R.W. Fus rejoined for Temp: duty.	
"	14.		"	
"	15.		"	
"	16.		"	
"	17.		"	
"	18.		"	
"	19.		"	
"	20.		"	
"	21.		Voluntary Church Parade.	

Army Form C. 2118.

WAR DIARY
or
INTELLIGENCE SUMMARY

(Erase heading not required.) 7th Bn. KING'S (Liverpool) REGT.

2nd Sheet

Instructions regarding War Diaries and Intelligence Summaries are contained in F. S. Regs., Part II. and the Staff Manual respectively. Title Pages will be prepared in manuscript.

Place	Date	Hour	Summary of Events and Information	Remarks and references to Appendices
PROVEN	July 1917 22.		Railway construction work carried on by Royal Engineers.	
"	23		" " " "	
"	24		" " " "	
"	25		" " " "	
"	26		" " " "	
"	27		" " " "	
"	28		Church Parade Service. 2nd Lt. E.T. Weadon joined for duty.	
"	29		Moved to Z Camp. Relieved by a Brigade.	
Z Camp	30		} Platoon Training	
"	31			

C.K. Potts. Lieut Colonel.
Comdg 7th Bn. Kings (Liverpool) Regt.

2449 Wt. W14957/M90 750,000 1/16 J.B.C. & A. Forms/C.2118/12.

55

1/7 Liverpool Regt

Vol XIII

March 1916

9e

Army Form C. 2118

WAR DIARY
or
INTELLIGENCE SUMMARY

(Erase heading not required.)

pl. Sheet. 9th Kings (Liverpool) Regt.

Instructions regarding War Diaries and Intelligence Summaries are contained in F.S. Regs., Part II. and the Staff Manual respectively. Title Pages will be prepared in manuscript.

Place	Date	Hour	Summary of Events and Information	Remarks and references to Appendices
MAILLY	1/4/16		Working parties	
"	2 "		"	
"	3 "		"	
"	4 "		Relieved 9th Kings in Front-line Trenches	
TRENCHES	5 "		In Trenches	
"	6 "		"	
"	7 "		"	
"	8 "		Relieved by 9th Kings and marched back to Beaumetz	
Beaumetz	9 "		Cleaning & equipment, Inspection and forming working parties	
"	10 "		Working parties	
"	11 "		"	
"	12 "		"	
"	13 "		"	
"	14 "		Left Beaumetz and relieved 9th Kings in Front-line Trenches	
Trenches	15 "		In Trenches 3.270 Stokes [mortars] killed	
"	16 "		" 18.32 PM mortar killed Capt J.G. Thompson slightly wounded	
"	17 "		" 1 man wounded	
"	18 "		nothing unusual	

1875 Wt. W593/826 1,000,000 4/15 J.B.C.,& A. A.D.S.S./Forms/C. 2118.

Army Form C. 2118

WAR DIARY
or
INTELLIGENCE SUMMARY

(Erase heading not required.) 9th Kings (Liverpool) Regt.

2nd Sheet

Place	Date	Hour	Summary of Events and Information	Remarks and references to Appendices
TRENCHES	19/7/15		Trenches heavily shelled 3 men killed 5 of 7 platoon Reserve & 3 of 5 platoon 1927 OM Ackherson 4 men wounded. Lieut W.J. Copeland wounded	
"	20"		Relief from trenches by 9th Kings. Proceeded to W.31.C.4.4 in support.	
VALLEY	21"		Working parties	
"	22"		" "	
"	23"		" "	
"	24"		" "	
"	25"		" "	
"	26"		Relieved 9 K Kings in front line trenches	
TRENCHES	27"		In Trenches	
"	28"		" "	
"	29"		" "	
"	30"		" "	
"	31"		" "	

Edwards N.
Lieut Colonel.
Comdg 9th Kings (Liverpool) Regt.

WAR DIARY
4th King's African Rifles
Regt.

March 1916

War Diary
of the
1/7 Liverpool R.
for the period
1st to 31st March,
1917.

SECRET AND CONFIDENTIAL

WAR DIARY.

For the month of

March 1917.

1/1st Bn. 'The Kings' (Lpool Regt).

Army Form C. 2118.

WAR DIARY
or
INTELLIGENCE SUMMARY
(Erase heading not required.) 1/4th Bn. The Kings. (L'pool Regt.) T.F.

ft Street

Place	Date	Hour	Summary of Events and Information	Remarks and references to Appendices
YPRES	March 1917 1.		Coy Training & working Parties	
"	2.		"	
"	3.		" relieved 9th Kings in trenches near Railway Wood	
TRENCHES	4.		Manned Trench Routine	
"	5.		"	
"	6.		"	
"	7.		" Relieved by 1/10 Scottish (K.L.R) and moved by Rail & 'Erie' to B. Camp.	
B. Camp.	8.		Cleaning up and Inspection	
"	9.		Coy Training	
"	10.		Church Parade & inspection	
"	11.		Coy Training. Baths.	
"	12.		"	
"	13.		"	
"	14.		Bde Ceremonial Parade. Gen'l Smyth presented with M.C. Gds Dunham L/Cpl Walton Br.S.Mrd Drummond & Drum-Sergt With Mily medals.	
"	15.		Coy Training	
"	16.		" Relieved 9th Kings in YPRES	
YPRES	17.		Church Parade & working parties	
"	18.		"	
"	19.		Training & working parties	
"	20.		"	
"	21.		" Relieved 9th Kings in Trenches	

Over

Army Form C. 2118.

WAR DIARY
or
INTELLIGENCE SUMMARY
(Erase heading not required.)

2nd Sheet

Place	Date	Hour	Summary of Events and Information	Remarks and references to Appendices
Trenches November 1917	22		Normal Trench Routine	
"	23		"	
"	24		"	
"	25		"	
"	26		Fighting patrol tried to cut or hang into Enemy Trenches and were overcome by Enemy. 1 man missing. Relieved by 9 K.R.R. and went to Billets in YPRES	
YPRES	27		"	
"	28		"	
"	29		"	
"	30		" " "	
"	31		Usual working parties &c.	

C.R. Attlee Lieut-Colonel
Comdg 17th Bn. The King's (Lpool Rgt) T.F.

Army Form C. 2118.

WAR DIARY
or
INTELLIGENCE SUMMARY

(Erase heading not required.) 1/7 K.R.R. The King's (Liverpool Regt.)

Instructions regarding War Diaries and Intelligence Summaries are contained in F. S. Regs., Part II. and the Staff Manual respectively. Title Pages will be prepared in manuscript.

Place	Date	Hour	Summary of Events and Information	Remarks and references to Appendices
Z Camp	Feby 1917 1.		Training	
"	2.		"	
"	3.		Church Parade. Inspection	
"	4.		Training	
"	5.		"	
"	6.		"	
"	7.		"	
"	8.		"	
"	9.		"	
"	10.		Church Parade. Inspection	
"	11.		Training	
"	12.		"	
"	13.		"	
"	14.		Inspection by Brigadier General Conevy. Brigade moved to YPRES. Knot & POPERINGHE Rail & YPRES.	
"	15.		Relieved 16th Rifle Bde. in Left sub-sector J Railway Wood sector.	
YPRES	16.		received 16th Kings.	
TRENCHES	17.		Trenches. usual routine	
"	18.		"	
"	19.		"	
"	20.		"	

Army Form C. 2118.

WAR DIARY
or
INTELLIGENCE SUMMARY

(Erase heading not required.)

2nd Sheet. 1/7th Bn The King's (Liverpool Regt)

Place	Date	Hour	Summary of Events and Information	Remarks and references to Appendices
TRENCHES	Feby 1917 22.		Relieved in Trenches by 8th Kings (shack) & moved back to Bulldozer YPRES.	
YPRES	" 23.		⎫	
"	" 24.		⎪	
"	" 25.		⎬ Working Parties. Coy. Training. Specialists Training.	
"	" 26.		⎪ Improvement of Billets etc.	
"	" 27.		⎪	
"	" 28.		⎭	

J.R. Smyth Captain
Comdg 1/7th Bn. The King's (Liverpool Regt)

2/3/1917.

CONFIDENTIAL

War Diary

of

1/7 Liverpool Regt.

for the period

1st to 28th February 1917

CONFIDENTIAL

Vol 26

War Diary
of
1/7th Liverpool R.
for the period
1st April to 30th April, 1917.

Army Form C. 2118.

WAR DIARY
or
INTELLIGENCE SUMMARY

(Erase heading not required.) 1/7th Bn KING'S (LPOOL REGT) T.F.

Instructions regarding War Diaries and Intelligence Summaries are contained in F. S. Regs., Part II. and the Staff Manual respectively. Title Pages will be prepared in manuscript.

2d Sheet.

Place	Date Hour	Summary of Events and Information	Remarks and references to Appendices
YPRES	April 1917 1.	Training and working parties. Relieved 9th L'pool Kings in Right Sub. Sector.	
TRENCHES	2.	Trenches. Usual Routine	
"	3.	" " "	
"	4.	" " "	
"	5.	" " "	
"	6.	" " "	
"	7.	Relieved by 10th Scottish Kings (Lpool Regt), and move by Rail to B Camp	
B. Camp	8.	Church Parade & Inspections	
"	9.	Moved to Z Camp.	
Z. Camp	10.	Training & Bathing	
"	11.	" " "	
"	12.	" " "	
"	13.	" " "	
"	14.	" " "	
"	15.	Church Parade and Inspection	
"	16.	Tactical scheme in morning, moved to YPRES S in the evening, & relieved 10th Scottish Bn.	
YPRES	17.	A & B Coys relieved 2 Coys 1/5th Royal North Lancs in Left Subsector of Railway Wood Section. C & D Coys remained at YPRES S. Bn Head Qrs at POT IJZE	
Trenches	18.	} Usual Trench Routine. The 2 Coys at YPRES S. Rested.	
"	19.		
"	20.		
"	21.		
"	22.		

Army Form C. 2118.

WAR DIARY
or
INTELLIGENCE SUMMARY

(Erase heading not required.) 1/7 Bn The Kings (L'pool Regt) T.F.

2nd Sheet.

Place	Date	Hour	Summary of Events and Information	Remarks and references to Appendices
TRENCHES ECOLE	April/17 23.		Relieved by 6th Bn The Kings (L'pool Regt) T.F and moved to the ECOLE.	
"	24.		⎫	
"	25.		⎬ Platoon Training, Working Parties & 300 men Bathed.	
"	26.		⎭	
"	27.			
"	28.			
"	29.		Church Parade. Working Parties. Relieved 9th Kings in the Right Section of Railway Wood Section.	
TRENCHES	30.		Mutual Trench Routine.	

C.R.Pyttu Lieut-Colonel
Comdg 1/7 Bn The Kings (L'pool Regt) T.F.

CONFIDENTIAL

War Diary
of
1/7th Liverpool R.
for the period
May 1st to 31st, 1917

Army Form C. 2118.

WAR DIARY
or
INTELLIGENCE SUMMARY
(Erase heading not required.) 1/7TH BN THE KINGS (LPOOL REGT)

1st SHEET.

Place	Date	Hour	Summary of Events and Information	Remarks and references to Appendices
Trenches.	May 1917 1.		Usual Trench Routine	
R.Sub Sector	2.		"	
Railway Wood	3.		"	
	4.		"	
	5.		Enemy blew in by enemy at 4.20 a.m. H.Q Hant-Reach by sniper. Relieved at night by 6thKings 1 Coy to Proven HQ Bn Camp. Church Parades	
B.Camp.	6.			
"	7.			
"	8.			
"	9.		Coys at training. Working parties YBattn of men	
"	10.		"	
"	11.		"	
Trenches	12.		Entrained at BRANDHOEK for YPRES and relieved the 9.Kings. 2 Coys in front line Tigerpole and 2 in YPRES.	
Ypres.	13.		Trench Routine. Working Parties.	
"	14.		"	

A6945 Wt.W1422/M1160 35,000 12/16 D.D.&L. Forms/C./2118/14.

Army Form C. 2118.

WAR DIARY
or
INTELLIGENCE SUMMARY.

(Erase heading not required.) 17 B/ The Kings (L'pool Regt)

Instructions regarding War Diaries and Intelligence Summaries are contained in F. S. Regs., Part II. and the Staff Manual respectively. Title pages 2nd Sheet will be prepared in manuscript.

Place	Date	Hour	Summary of Events and Information	Remarks and references to Appendices
Trenches YPRES	April 1917 15.		Trench routine & working parties	
"	16.		"	
"	17.		"	
"	18.		Relieved by 10th Scottish moved by Rail to POPERINGHE & Billeted in the HOPSTORE	
POPERINGHE	19.		"	
BOLLEZEELE	20.		Moved by Rail to WATTEN thence by Road to BOLLEZEELE. Church parades, kit inspection & cleaning up	
"	21.			
"	22.			
"	23.		Coy & Battalion training	
"	24.			
"	25.			
"	26.			
"	27.		Church Parade. Kit inspection & Battalion Sports	
"	28.		Coy & Battalion training & Brigade Sports.	
"	29.		"	
"	30.		"	
"	31.		"	

C.H. Potter Lieut-Colonel
Commanding 17 Kings (L'pool Regt)

Vol 28

24c

CONFIDENTIAL

War Diary
of
1/7th Liverpool R.
for the period
June 1st to June 30th, 1917

Army Form C. 2118.

WAR DIARY
or
INTELLIGENCE SUMMARY.
(Erase heading not required.)

Instructions regarding War Diaries and Intelligence Summaries are contained in F. S. Regs., Part II. and the Staff Manual respectively. Title pages will be prepared in manuscript.

Place	Date	Hour	Summary of Events and Information	Remarks and references to Appendices
BOLLEZEELE	1917 June 1+2		Training	
- do -	3rd		Church Parade	
- do -		4.69	Training	
- do -		10.15	Church Parade	
- do -		11.15	Training	
- do -		12.45	Battalion marched to H.1.a (BELGIUM Sheet 28 N.W.) Dispositions A Coy L4. and by road to ESQUELBECQ; thence by train to POPERINGHE C Coy + 2 Platoons D Coy. P1. 2 Platoons D Coy YPRES, B Coy + B.H.Q. H1a. Working Parties	
MERSEY CAMP 13-22nd H.1.a				
- do -	23rd		Moved to DERBY CAMP (H.1.c). Working Parties	
DERBY CAMP	24th	6.30"	Working Parties	
H.1.c				

Sh. Williams
Major
Comdg 1/4th Bn "Sherwood (Ford. Regt.) SR

Vol 29

25-c

War Diary
of the
1/7 Liverpool R.
for the period
1st July to 31st July,
1917.

SECRET & CONFIDENTIAL

War Diary

for the month of

July 1917.

1/7th Bn. "The Kings" (L'pool Regt).

WAR DIARY
INTELLIGENCE SUMMARY

Army Form C. 2118.

1st Sheet 1/7 KB N THE KINGS (LPOOL REGT) T.F

Place	Date July 1917	Hour	Summary of Events and Information	Remarks and references to Appendices
DERBY CAMP	1st		Moved to WESTBECOURT	
WESTBECOURT	2		⎫	
"	3		⎬ Company Training	
"	4		⎪	
"	5		⎭	
"	6		Moved to MORINGHEM	
MORINGHEM	7		Training	
"	8		Church Parade	
"	9		Training	
"	10		Attack Practice on Taped area	
"	11		Training	
"	12		Brigade attack Practice	
"	13		"	
"	14		Battalion Training	
"	15		Brigade Church Parade	
"	16		Brigade attack Practice	

Army Form C. 2118.

WAR DIARY
or
INTELLIGENCE SUMMARY

(Erase heading not required.) 1/7th Bn. King's (L'pool Regt) T.F.

2nd Sheet

Instructions regarding War Diaries and Intelligence Summaries are contained in F.S. Regs, Part II. and the Staff Manual respectively. Title Pages will be prepared in manuscript.

Place	Date	Hour	Summary of Events and Information	Remarks and references to Appendices
MORINGHEM	July 17, 1917	.	Attack practise with 9th King's Brigade attack practise.	
"	18	.	"	
"	19	.	C.O. Inspection and Company lectures.	
"	20	.	"	
"	21	.	Moved to B. Camp via St. Omer and Poperinghe. In the evening A & D Coys moved to Durham Redoubt Ramparts at Ypres.	
"	22	.	B " " " "	
"	23	.	C " " Prison Vicinity	
on detailed for sp.	24	.	H.Q. & B Coy remained at B. Camp.	
	25	.	} Furnished working parties as detailed.	
Trenches	26	.	Relieved 5th Kings in Potijze Sector.	
"	27	.	} Holding front-line system.	
"	28	.		
"	29	.	Relieved by 5th Kings in Potijze Sector & Bn. moved as follows: H.Q. & D Coy in Potijze Road Dugouts. B in Ramparts C in Magazine.	
	30	.	Moved into assembly position for operation on 31st.	
	31	.	Operation. See attached operation orders & narrative.	

C.R. Pitt.
Lieut-Colonel
Commdg. 1/7th Bn. The King's (L'pool Regt) T.F.

SECRET. Copy to......

OPERATION ORDER No. 93,
By Lieut-Colonel C.K. POTTER,
Comdg, 1/7th Bn "The King's (L'pool Regiment).

In the Field   THURSDAY   26th July 1917.

Reference Map
    Attached Trench Sketch Map

1. INTENTION, INFORMATION, and OBJECTIVES (See 165th Infantry Brigade Operation Order No. 125, paras 1,2,3,4,5,)
The OBJECTIVE allotted to the Battalion is that part of the FREZENBERG Line from D.19.c.75.85 through POMMERN REDOUBT to D.19.a.30.38 and the consolidation of the "Black Line" from D.19.c.90.94 to D.19.a.45.50.

The OBJECTIVES allotted to Companies are:-

"A" COMPANY:- From D.19.c.75.85 to D.19.a.67.05 including Communication Trench to IBERIAN. An advanced Bombing Section followed by a Lewis Gun Section will be pushed forward to IBERIAN, which they will capture and hold.

"D" COMPANY. 1st objective D.19.a.52.02 to D.19a.12.28.
            2nd   ,,   D.19.a.52.02 to D.19.a.30.28.
with a Bombing Section on Right going forward to get in touch with "A" Company.

"B" Company 1st Objective D.19.a.60.02 to D.19.a.45.40.
           2nd   D.19.a.37.45 to D.19.a.55.40.
throwing back left flank from each objective to get into touch with "D" Company.

"C" Company:- PLUM REDOUBT, D.24.d.21.00 to D.24.c.85.30

2. FORMATION:- (See Brigade Operation Order No. 125 para 6)
The Battalion will be formed up in OXFORD TRENCH behind WARWICK FARM astride the STRAND on a frontage of 350 Yards. This position will be taken up on Y/Z night, the Companies moving, "A" and "D" Companies from POTIJZE ROAD DUGOUTS, "B" Coy from the RAMPARTS and "C" Company from the MAGAZINE, YPRES. Movement to be made by Section half Platoons at 100 Yards distance. All movement East of JUNCTION ROAD to be completed by 9-30 p.m. Order for crossing JUNCTION ROAD:- "A" "D" "B" and "C" Coys. "A" Company to move at 8-15 p.m. "D" Company at 8-30 p.m. "B" Company at 8-15 p.m. "C" Company at 8-25 p.m.
(will be notified later)
At ZERO plus 15 Minutes the Battalion will leave WARWICK TRENCH and OXFORD ROAD so as to pass over the "BLUE LINE" at ZERO plus 1 hour 15 Minutes.

The Battalion will advance as already practiced.

"A" Company in 2 waves on right with Right Flank on Brigade Boundary on a frontage of 175 Yards.

"D" Company in 2 waves on left with left flank on Yellow Line as shown in the attached map on a frontage of 175 Yards.

At ZERO "A" and "D" Companies with Moppers Up of "C" Company will move forward to WARWICK TRENCH.

-2-

"C" Company, 3 Platoons as Moppers Up for PLUM REDOUBT with first waves of leading Companies. 1 Platoon with 3rd and 4th waves on Right. All Platoons of "C" Company will stop at PLUM REDOUBT, except as otherwise ordered, and will be the Battalion reserve.

"B" Company will form 3rd and 4th waves on left.

Lines will move at 20 paces distance. Waves will move at 100 Yards paces distance. On approaching the objectives Waves will close up to not more than 40 paces distance. On arrival at the "BLUE LINE", the leading wave will close up to Barrage, which will be stationary 300 Yards in front of Blue Line until ZERO plus 1 hour 23 Minutes, when it will advance in jumps of 100 Yards every 4 Minutes.

BATTALION HEADQUARTERS will be established:-
   1st phase   WARWICK FARM.
   2nd   ,,   On Advance from "BLUE LINE" at UHLAN FARM.
   3rd   ,,   On consolidation of "BLACK LINE" at POMMERN CASTLE.

3. ARTILLERY BARRAGE
As per 165 Infantry Brigade Operation Order No.125 para 8, and map issued.

4. TANKS.
Six Tanks will co-operate with the Brigade in the attack on the "BLACK LINE". They will normally operate between first wave and the Barrage and will at once engage any hostile Machine Gun which opens fire. Companies must not be diverted from their proper direction by following the Tanks. The Infantry must on no account wait for the Tanks,; they must keep close behind the Barrage whether the Tanks are there or not.

5. MACHINE GUNS
See 165 Infantry Brigade Operation Order No. 125 para 10.

6. TRENCH MORTARS.
See 165th Infantry Brigade Operation Order No. 125 para 11. The selected place for the two Guns with the Battalion is D.19,a,28.12. Every Officer in the Battalion must know where the Stokes Mortars are to be found.

7. Action of Infantry and Trench Mortars against pockets of Germans:
See 165 Infantry Brigade Operation Order No. 125, para 12

8. CONSOLIDATION.
  a. "A" Company will construct a strong Point at S.E. Corner of the POMMERN REDOUBT to protect the right flank. The Garrison will be at least 1 Platoon.
  b. "B" Company will construct and occupy the strong Point on spur between POMMERN REDOUBT and GALLIPOLI* with 1 Platoon 2 Lewis Guns and 2 Machine Guns. Observation etc as per last sub-para in para 13 of Brigade Operation Order No. 125.

See 165 Infantry Brigade Operation Order No. 125 para 13.

9. STRONG POINT constructed by the R.E's at about D.19.c.05.60 will be garrisoned by half a Platoon and 1 Lewis Gun of "C" Company on receipt of orders from B.H.Q.

* at D.19. b. 00. 40 commanding ground to North and North East.

10. **S.O.S. SIGNAL.**
S.O.S. Signal will be the Rifle Grenade pattern bursting into 2 red and 2 Green. These signals will be carried by Officers.

11. **FLARES.** Will be lit behind cover or at the bottom of a trench when possible. They will only be lit by men in the most advanced positions reached, they must on no account be lit by men behind. The signal for lighting the flares will be a White Very Light fired from an aeroplane. This will probably be preceded by a KLAXON HORN to draw attention to the aeroplane.
Watson FANS will also be issued for Signalling to aeroplanes.

12. **PROTECTION OF FLANKS.**
See 165 Infantry Brigade Operation Order No. 125 para 17 "C" Company will establish a defensive flank along CAMEL AVENUE from the BLUE LINE to the Road running from FREZENBERG past SQUARE FARM. The attention of "A" Company is drawn to SMOKE Barrage.

13. **PRISONERS.**
The instructions contained in para 18 of 165 Infantry Brigade Operation Order No. 125 will be strictly adhered to as regards prisoners.

14. **CARE OF MEN.**
It is of the utmost importance that men should get as much rest as possible. All men not actually required to work should be allotted dugouts when available and be allowed to rest undisturbed.

15. **DRESS**
See Appendix 1.

16. **COMMUNICATIONS:-**
Communication will be maintained until a cable is laid forward to Companies.
Posts are being established at UHLAN FARM, PLUM FARM POMMERN CASTLE.
Special instructions have been issued to the Battalion Signalling Officer.
See also 165 Infantry Brigade Operation Order No. 125 para 21.

17. **REPORTS.**
After the capture of an objective reports are required on the following points when applicable.-

Exact position, and if in touch with troops on flank. Condition of trench. Amount of cover etc. Action and position of neighbouring troops. Position of hostile barrage. Condition of C.T's. Number and position of dugouts and accommodation, and whether shell proof. Approximate casualties. Prisoners or captured Machine Guns.

18. **LIAISON.**
O.C. "A" Company will maintain touch with the Battalion on the Right (10/11th K.L.I.) and "B" Company will also maintain touch with 9th King's on his left and "D" Coy with the 9th King's on the Left.

19. **PACK ANIMALS**
Pack animals will be utilised to send up S.A.A. Bombs etc as soon as the Black Line is captured.

18. LIAISON
O.C. "A" Coy will establish Liaison Posts at C.30.b.60.95 and D.19.c.70.75 with 10/11th Bn H.L.I.   "B" and "D" coys will also maintain touch with 9th King's on the left.

-4-

20. TRAFFIC and POSTS.

After ZERO the STRAND will be an up TRENCH and PAGODA a down Trench. If the enemy's Artillery fire is not heavy all movement after Zero will be over the top. The following Straggler Posts will be established:-

    a.   Junction of OXFORD TRENCH with STRAND.
    b.   Junction of OXFORD TRENCH and PAGODA TRENCH.
    c.   Junction of OXFORD TRENCH and LONE TRENCH.

(a) Posts will be found by the 5th King's, (b and c) by 6th King's. Posts will consist of 1 N.C.O. and 2 men. Posts A and b will also watch tracks No. 4 and 5 respectively. No unwounded man is to be allowed to pass these posts except runners and stretcher bearers. Men suffering from Shell Shock or Gas will not be allowed to pass. All unauthorised men trying to pass these posts will have their names taken and will then be collected in OXFORD TRENCH near the STRAND. They will be available for carrying parties.
Divisional Brigade Posts will be established at I.4.b.25.70 and I.4.a.42.85, each Post consisting of 2 Regimental Police of 7th King's. Instructions have been issued by the Division to these posts.

21. DUMPS.

The following Battalion Dump has been established by the Brigade at the Junction of OXFORD TRENCH and STRAND, and contains S.A.A. Bombs, Water, R.E. material etc.
This will be in charge of Sergt Edwards and 2 men.

22. SALVAGE.

No damage is to be done to captured guns or machine guns unless there appears to be a likelihood of their re-capture by the enemy. All captured rations, water tins, bombs and R.E. material will be collected in dumps and issued to troops as required under Battalion arrangements. All papers, maps etc which may be found in dugouts or on German Officers will be collected and sent to Battalion Headquarters. All maps and photos will be collected from our own casualties when possible and sent to Battalion Headquarters for re-distribution

23. MEDICAL.

See Appendix 2.

24. WATER, TEA etc

See Appendix 3.

25. SURPLUS KIT.

See Appendix 4.

26. MAPS.

All Officer in the Attack will carry the following maps and message forms:-
    a.   ST JULIEN 1/10,000 ordinary trench map.
        ZONNEBEKE   "   "
        WESTROOSEBEKE "   "
    b.   FREZENBERG 1/10,000 brief size trench map.
    c.   Barrage Map- showing the movement of the barrage, Strong Points, supporting Points, liaison points etc
    d.   An adequate number of message forms with map on the back
The above will be issued later.

27. ZERO Hour will be notified later.

ACKNOWLEDGE.

F. Toole Captain
ADJT. 7TH BN THE KING'S (L'POOL) REGT.

APPENDIX 1.

DRESS.

Fighting Order, with Packs instead of Haversacks.

The following Bombs, Flares etc will be carried:-

LEWIS GUNNERS:-
- 1 extra Iron Ration.
- 3 Sandbags
- 2 Mill's Bombs
- 1 extra Water Bottle containing Tea

BOMBERS:-
- 1 extra Iron Ration.
- 3 Sandbags
- 12 Mill's Bombs
- 1 extra water bottle containing Tea

RIFLE BOMBERS:-
- 6 No.23's or No 24's Rifle Bombs.
  The men carrying Grenade Rifles will carry No. 24's and the remainder of the Teams No. 23's.
- 3 Sandbags
- 2 Bombs.
- 1 extra Iron Ration.
- 1 extra Water Bottle containing Tea.

RIFLEMEN:-
- 3 Sandbags
- 2 Mill's Bombs.
- 1 extra Iron Ration.
- 1 extra Water Bottle, containing Tea

No. 2 Lewis Gunners will carry 4 magazines. Remaining magazines up to 30 will be distributed equally amongst the Platoon. The extra 14 magazines per Gun will be stored at POTIJZE DUMP.

	"A"	"B"	"C"	"D"
Picks	15	15	15	15
Shovels	60	60	60	60
Smoke Bombs	25	25	-	-
S.O.S. Signals	10	10	-	10
Very Lights 1"	60	50	-	5
White Flares	100	100	20	50
S.O.S. Rifle Rockets	5	5	-	2
Smoke Candles	A 75	B -	C 25	D -

The S.O.S. Signals will be carried by Officers.

APPENDIX 2.

MEDICAL ARRANGEMENTS.

(a) Regimental Aid Posts at ZERO:-
   C.24.c.6.7. (Pagoda Street) for 2 attacking Battalions.
   Prior to assault the supporting Battalions will share these Aid Posts.

(b) Collecting Posts d.27.d.5.1. (Junction Road)
   I.4.a.7.3. (POTIJZE)

(c) ADVANCED Dressing Station, I.1.b.9.5. (Canal Bank)

Walking wounded via BAGDAD STREET and GORDON STREETS to Collecting Posts at POTIJZE and ST JEAN.

Appendix 2 (Contd)

Walking wounded, via PAGODA STREET and GORDEN STREET to Collecting Posts at POTIJZE and ST JEAN.

Any unwounded enemy that may be taken will be used to carry and help our wounded down to the Dressing Station. A reserve Stretcher Bearer will be earmarked in each Platoon to assist the wounded, if necessary, after all objectives have been gained.

All walking wounded will carry their arms and equipment and to be in charge of Prisoners (if any)

APPENDIX 3.

WATER, TEA etc.

The extra water bottle filled with Tea on X Day will be carried in the Pack

Breakfast will be made in the "Y" day area late in the evening and carried up in Thermos Cans.

Water to fill No. 1 Water Bottle will be supplied from Water Cart on Y Day and night.

The Quartermaster will send Cocoa up with "Y" Day Rations.

The attention of all ranks is drawn to the necessity of returning Empty Petrol Tins; unless this is done the supply of water cannot be guaranteed.

APPENDIX 4.

SURPLUS KIT.

Each man has been provided with a sandbag and tally. The Greatcoat, Haversack, personal effects and spare kit will be put in the sandbag, securely tied and properly labelled. The sandbag will be deposited at the Dump at POTIJZE at the time the men receive their Bombs, Rifle Bombs, extra day's ration etc

A Guard of 1 N.C.O. and 2 men will be found by "C" Company [from the men] who are to be left out of the operations.

"A" and "D" Coy will go to the dump by parties of 4 during morning of "Y" day, deposit their kit and receive stores to be carried.

"B" and "C" Coys will file past the Dump on their way to OXFORD ROAD, deposit surplus kit and receive stores to be carried.

1/7th Battalion, "The King's" (Liverpool Regiment) T.F.

CASUALTY LIST (To be attached to A.F.B 213 dated 3-8-17)

-o-o-o-o-o-

KILLED IN ACTION

269166	Pte	Jackson K.	"A"	30-7-17
268951	"	Power L.	"A"	30-7-17
265632	Cpl	Howard J	"A"	1-8-17
265974	L/C	Makinson, M.	"A"	31-7-17
266923	"	Moore R.	"A"	31-7-17
267324	Pte	Rooney, P	"A"	1-8-17
267893	"	Archer, F.	"A"	31-7-17
268421	"	Wooley W.	"A"	31-7-17
266774	"	Williamson W	"A"	1-8-17
268918	"	Bourne F.T.	"A"	31-7-17
268440	"	Lee T.	"A"	1-8-17
269347	"	Cruikshanks J.	"A"	1-8-17
265249	Cpl	Gill J.	"A"	31-7-17
265731	Sgt	Stockton C.A.	"B"	31-7-17
265246	Cpl	Wright J.	"B"	~~1-8-17~~ 31-7-17
265080	Pte	Kimmer R.B.	"B"	31-7-17
266126	"	Gough J	"B"	31-7-17
268413	"	Stevens J.H.	"B"	2-8-17
268430	"	Braddock W	"B"	31-7-17
265226	"	Brennen, E.	"B"	2-8-17
265203	"	Leatherbarrow J.	"B"	1-8-17 — attd H.Q. Coy R.E.
265765	Sgt	Robinson, W	"C"	31-7-17
267366	Pte	Bennett, F	"C"	31-7-17
268944	"	Hesketh, J.	"C"	2-8-17
268718	"	Kemp, H.	"C"	2-8-17
266239	"	O'Brien, E.	"D"	31-7-17
265965	"	Lloyd H.	"D"	31-7-17
265739	L/C	Carter B	"D"	1-8-17
267420	Pte	Gaskell T	"D"	1-8-17
268528	"	Lord J.W.	"D"	1-8-17
267625	Pte	Green, C.	"D"	31-7-17
267907	"	Robson R.	"D"	31-7-17

Casualty List Sheet 2.

WOUNDED IN ACTION

265382	Sgt McQuillen A.	"A"	31-7-17
265932	Cpl Routledge J.	"A"	31-7-17
266662	L/C Santos J.	"A"	31-7-17
265604	L/C Scardwood G.E.	"A"	31-7-17
265925	L/C Hiers J.	"A"	31-7-17
268635	L/C Monk J	"A"	31-7-17
267301	Pte Alty R	"A"	31-7-17
265329	Pte Thomas D.	"A"	31-7-17
268682	" Greaves D.	"A"	31-7-17
267636	" Tyler J.	"A"	1-8-17
265602	" Jackson W	"A"	31-7-17
300020	" Gorman S	"A"	31-7-17
303604	" Mellor P	"A"	2-8-17
267536	" Dickenson A.	"A"	1-8-17
265230	" Brooks J.	"A"	31-7-17
265630	" Craig A.	"A"	31-7-17
239301	" Convey P.	"A"	1-8-17
267622	" Fox R.	"A"	31-7-17
268440	" Billington A.	"A"	31-7-17
265545	" Shaw W.	"A"	31-7-17
262920	" Flanagan	"A"	31-7-17
267270	" Clarke G	"A"	31-7-17
265981	" Holt J.	"A"	1-8-17
266997	" McDowell D	"A"	1-8-17
266619	" Power R.	"A"	31-7-17
268418	" Billington S.	"A"	31-7-17
267654	" Quayle G.	"A"	31-7-17
269747	" McKay T.H.	"A"	31-7-17
267139	" Stevens L.	"A"	31-7-17
267135	" Peterson O.	"A"	31-7-17
267639	" Gannon O.	"A"	31-7-17
267735	" Wheeler E.	"A"	31-7-17
267695	" Birdwhistle E.	"A"	1-8-17
49872	Sgt Hernot H	"A"	30-7-17
265465	Pte Mitchell T.	"A"	30-7-17
260987	" Moreland A.	"A"	30-7-17
269367	" McGuire J.	"A"	30-7-17
267167	" Summers E.	"A"	30-7-17
267780	" Hicks W.C.	"A"	30-7-17
265577	L/C Lloyd W.	"C"	31-7-17
267644	S/C Satterall F.	"C"	31-7-17
268635	Pte Norwood R.	"C"	31-7-17
268845	" Heeding W	"C"	31-7-17
265716	" Humphries G.	"C"	2-8-17
265656	" Allman W.	"C"	31-7-17
265809	" Burns R.	"C"	31-7-17
331409	" Dangerfield G.	"C"	31-7-17
269253	" Dawson D.	"C"	28-7-17
268445	" Parley J.	"C"	31-7-17
268452	" Fitzgerald J	"C"	31-7-17
267904	" Kenyon S.	"C"	31-7-17
266536	" Morrigan P.	"C"	31-7-17
267186	" McCready E.	"C"	3-8-17
265467	" McAvoy M.	"C"	2-8-17
268633	" Bury J.	"C"	31-7-17
268465	" Owens G.	"C"	31-7-17
268165	" Peterson J.	"C"	31-7-17
267777	" Prescott J.	"C"	31-7-17
267951	" Rimmer P.	"C"	31-7-17
268216	" Rogers W.	"C"	31-7-17
268186	" Thorp W.	"C"	31-7-17
268439	" Williams J.	"C"	1-8-17

Casualty List (Sheet 3)

WOUNDED IN ACTION.

308336	Pte	MacDonald R	"C"	31-7-17	Died of wounds 1-8-17
265545	CSM	Wilkins, F	"C"	31-7-17	
265178	Pte	Hewitt J.	"C"	1-8-17	
266720	Sgt	Harrington D.R.	"D"	1-8-17	
266814	Cpl	Quaile, W.	"D"	2-8-17	
269243	Pte	Ashworth, W.	"D"	31-7-17	
266919	"	Griffiths, R.	"D"	31-7-17	
267601	"	Kelly, J.J.	"D"	31-7-17	
301768	"	Hewitt, W	"D"	1-8-17	
267246	"	Brew, A	"D"	31-7-17	
268540	"	Mellor F	"D"	31-7-17	
265936	"	Barrett S	"D"	31-7-17	
265922	"	Sgt Sherwood S.J.G.	"D"	31-7-17	
266755	Pte	Balshaw J.	"D"	31-7-17	
265464	"	Gorrel, R.	"D"	31-7-17	
267782	"	Green G.	"D"	31-7-17	
266958	"	Villiers A.	"D"	31-7-17	
265794	"	Rimmer, T.	"D"	3-7-17	
266790	"	Rees S.J.L.	"D"	31-7-17	
267569	"	Howard, C.	"D"	31-7-17	
266333	"	Welsby J.	"D"	31-7-17	
268526	"	Doran W.	"D"	31-7-17	
267236	"	Pickering F.	"D"	31-7-17	
269323	"	Broughton H.	"D"	31-7-17	
267326	"	Jackson H	"D"	31-7-17	
265740	"	Blackhurst X	"D"	31-7-17	
265766	"	Edgar E.	"D"	31-7-17	
266035	"	Morris, W.	"D"	31-7-17	
265190	"	Doyle D.	"D"	31-7-17	
265051	L/S	Stafford J.	"D"	31-7-17	
267922	Sgt	Simpson H	"D"	31-7-17	
265473	Cpl	Wright J.	"D"	31-7-17	
266918	Pte	Brown G	"D"	31-7-17	
266668	"	Dean, J.	"D"	31-7-17	
267152	"	Dickenson A	"D"	31-7-17	
269285	"	Fletcher A.	"D"	31-7-17	
267908	"	Royle, J.	"D"	31-7-15	
267796	"	Williams W.C.	"D"	31-7-17	
267302	"	Siddall R.	"D"	31-7-17	
268812	"	Rodgers, J	"D"	31-7-17	
266972	"	Riley W.	"D"	31-7-17	
268444	"	Whitehead,	"D"	31-7-17	
265338	"	Milton F.	"D"	31-7-17	
266675	"	Waydock T.	"D"	2-8-17	
267313	Pte	Richardson F.	"B"	2-8-17	
267122	Sgt	Thompson J	"B"	31-7-17	
268577	Pte	Bairn J.	"B"	31-7-17	
267250	"	White T.	"B"	31-7-17	
266474	"	Cawley C.	"B"	31-7-17	
267348	"	Fallon, C.E.	"B"	31-7-17	
268488	"	Peck H.	"B"	31-7-17	
267616	"	Crossfield W.C.	"B"	31-7-17	
49835	"	Barton R.	"B"	31-7-17	
332243	"	Rice R.	"B"	31-7-17	
265858	"	Quigley J.	"B"	31-7-17	
49874	"	Bradley J.	"B"	31-7-17	
49847	"	Dee A.H.	"B"	31-7-17	
266497	"	O'Reilly J.	"B"	1-8-17	
49848	"	Doyle J.	"B"	31-7-17	

Casualty List (Sheet 4)

WOUNDED IN ACTION.

268544	L/C	Mallan P.	"B"	31-7-17
266492	Pte	Bishop J.	"B"	31-7-17
266366	"	Seddon R.	"B"	31-7-17
265278	Cpl	Jennions T.	"B"	31-7-17
49868	Pte	Gribble W.	"B"	31-7-17
266757	"	Aspinall D.	"B"	31-7-17
267349	"	Rothwell J.	"B"	31-7-17
269002	"	Keeling A.	"B"	31-7-17
267201	"	Denmon W.	"B"	31-7-17
268322	"	Hollis T.	"B"	31-7-17
267015	"	Jones C.G.	"B"	31-7-17
49863	"	Sinks W.	"B"	31-7-17
49857	"	Pitman J.H.	"B"	2-8-17
307346	"	Walton D.	"B"	2-8-17
49861	"	Willis A.J.	"B"	30-7-17
239289	"	Bull J.	"B"	30-7-17
268392	"	Sowden H	C	31-7-17
268558	"	Roche J.	C	31-7-17

S E C R E T.　　　　　　　　　　　　　　　　　　　　Copy No......

OPERATION ORDER NO. 93
by Lieut-Colonel C.K. POTTER,
COMDG, 1/7th Bn. "THE KING'S" (Liverpool Regt)

Reference Maps:- ST JULIEN 28 N.W. 1/10,000
　　　　　　　　　ZONNEBEKE 28 N.E. 1/10,000　　　　28th July 1917

1. INTENTION, INFORMATION and OBJECTIVES (see 165th Infantry Brigade Operation Order No. 125, paras 1,2,3,4,5)

    The OBJECTIVES allotted to the 7th King's is that part of the FREZENBERG Line from D.19.c.75.85 through POMMERN REDOUBT to D.19.a.30.38 and the consolidation of the "BLACK LINE" from D.19.c.90.94 to D.19.a.45.50.

    The OBJECTIVES allotted to Companies are:-

    "A" COMPANY:- From D.19.c.75.85 to D.19.a.67.05 including Communication Trench to IBERIAN. An Advanced Bombing Section followed by a Lewis Gun Section will be pushed forward to IBERIAN, which they will capture and hold.

    "D" COMPANY:- 1st Objective D.19.a.52.02 to D.19.a.12.28
    　　　　　　　 2nd　　 ,,　　D.19.a.52.02 to D.19.a.30.28.
    with a Bombing Section on Right going forward to get in touch with "A" Company.

    "B" Company:- 1st objective D.19.a.60.02 to D.19.a.45.40
    　　　　　　　 2nd　　 ,,　　D.19.a.67.05 to D.19.a.55.40
    throwing back left flank from each objective to get into touch with "D" Company.

    "C" COMPANY:- PLUM REDOUBT D.24.d.21.00 to D.24.c.85.30

2. FORMATION:- (See Brigade Operation Order No. 125 para 6)

    The Battalion will be formed up in the vicinity of OXFORD TRENCH behind WARWICK FARM, astride the STRAND on a frontage of 350 Yards. This position will be taken up on Y/Z night, the Companies moving "A" and "D" Companies from POTIJZE ROAD DUGOUTS, "B" Company from the RAMPARTS and "C" Company from the MAGAZINE, YPRES. Movement to be made by sections at 50 Yards distance. All movement east of JUNCTION ROAD to be completed by 9-30 p.m. ORDER for crossing JUNCTION ROAD:- "A" "D" "B" and "C" Coys "A" Company to move at 8-15 p.m. "D" Company at 8-30 p.m. "B" Company at 8-15 p.m. and "C" Company at 8-25 p.m.

    At ZERO "A" and "D" Companies with Moppers Up of "C" Company will move forward to WARWICK TRENCH.

    At ZERO plus X Minutes the Battalion will leave WARWICK TRENCH and OXFORD ROAD so as to pass over the "BLUE LINE" at ZERO plus 1 hour and 15 Minutes.　　[X will be notified later.]

    The Battalion will advance as already practiced.

    "A" Company in two waves on right with Right Flank on Brigade Boundary on a frontage of 175 Yards.

    "D" Company in 2 waves on left with left flank on YELLOW LINE as shown on the attached sketch map, on a frontage of 175 Yards

"O/C"

SECRET.   Copy No......

OPERATION ORDER NO. 93
by Lieut-Colonel C.K. POTTER,
COMDG, 1/7th Bn. "THE KING'S" (Liverpool Regt)

Reference Maps:-   ST JULIEN 28 N.W. 1/10,000
                    ZONNEBEKE 28 N.E. 1/10,000   28th July 1917

1. INTENTION, INFORMATION and OBJECTIVES (see 165th Infantry Brigade Operation Order No. 125, paras 1,2,3,4,5)

   The OBJECTIVES allotted to the 7th King's is that part of the FREZENBERG Line from D.19.c.75.85 through POMMERN REDOUBT to D.19.a.30.38 and the consolidation of the "BLACK LINE" from D.19.c.90.94 to D.19.a.45.50.

   The OBJECTIVES allotted to Companies are:-

   "A" COMPANY:- From D.19.c.75.85 to D.19.a.67.05 including Communication Trench to IBERIAN. An Advanced Bombing Section followed by a Lewis Gun Section will be pushed forward to IBERIAN, which they will capture and hold.

   "D" COMPANY:- 1st Objective D.19.a.52.02 to D.19.a.12.28
                 2nd   "   D.19.a.52.02 to D.19.a.30.28.
   with a Bombing Section on Right going forward to get in touch with "A" Company.

   "B" Company:- 1st objective D.19.a.60.02 to D.19.a.45.40
                 2nd   "   D.19.a.67.05 to D.19.a.55.40
   throwing back left flank from each objective to get into touch with "D" Company.

   "C" COMPANY:- PLUM REDOUBT D.24.d.21.00 to D.24.c.85.30

2. FORMATION:- (See Brigade Operation Order No. 125 para 6)

   The Battalion will be formed up in OXFORD TRENCH behind WARWICK FARM, astride the STRAND on a frontage of 350 Yards. This position will be taken up on Y/Z night, the Companies moving

   BOUNDARIES OF FORMING UP PLACES.
   Right Battalion Boundary will be C.29.c.40.08.
   Left Battalion Boundary will be C.28.d.86.56.

   ZE ROAD DUGOUTS, "B" Company from the MAGAZINE, YPRES. at 50 Yards distance. All to be completed by 9-30 p.m. :- "A" "D" "B" and "C" Coys "D" Company at 8-30 p.m. "B" Company at 8-15 p.m. and "C" Company at 8-25 p.m.

   At ZERO "A" and "D" Companies with Moppers Up of "C" Company will move forward to WARWICK TRENCH.

   At ZERO plus X Minutes the Battalion will leave WARWICK TRENCH and OXFORD ROAD so as to pass over the "BLUE LINE" at ZERO plus 1 hour and 15 Minutes.

   X will be notified later.

   The Battalion will advance as already practiced.

   "A" Company in two waves on right with Right Flank on Brigade Boundary on a frontage of 175 Yards.

   "D" Company in 2 waves on left with left flank on YELLOW LINE as shown on the attached sketch map, on a frontage of 175 Yards

-2-

"C" Company, 3 Platoons as Moppers up for PLUM REDOUBT with first waves of leading Companies. 1 Platoon with 3rd and 4th waves on right. All Platoons of "C" Company will stop at PLUM REDOUBT, except as otherwise ordered, and will be the Battalion reserve.

"B" Company will form 3rd and 4th waves on left.

Lines will move at 20 paces distance. Waves will move at 100 paces distance. On approaching the objectives waves will close up to not more than 40 paces distance. On arrival at the "BLUE LINE", the leading wave will close up to barrage, which will be stationary 300 Yards in front of "BLUE LINE" until ZERO plus 1 hour 23 Minutes, when it will advance in jumps of 100 Yards every 4 minutes.

BATTALION HEADQUARTERS will be established:-
 1st phase WARWICK FARM.
 2nd ,, On advance from "BLUE LINE" at UHLAN FARM.
 3rd phase On consolidation of "BLACK LINE" at POMMERN CASTLE.

3. ARTILLERY BARRAGE.
As per 165 Infantry Brigade Operation Order No. 125 para 8 and map issued.

4. TANKS.
6 Tanks will co-operate with the Brigade in the attack on the "BLACK LINE". They will normally operate between first wave and the barrage, and will at once engage any hostile machine gun which opens fire. Companies must not be diverted from their proper direction by following the Tanks. The Infantry must on no account wait for the Tanks; they must keep close behind the barrage whether the Tanks are there or not.

5. MACHINE GUNS.
See 165th Infantry Brigade Operation Order No.125, para 10.

6. TRENCH MORTARS.
See 165 Infantry Brigade Operation Order No. 125 para 11. The selected place for the two guns with the Battalion is D.19.a.28.12. Every Officer in the Battalion must know where the Stokes Mortars are to be found.

7. ACTION OF INFANTRY AND TRENCH MORTARS AGAINST POCKETS OF GERMANS. (See 165 Infantry Brigade Operation Order No. 125 para 12.

8. CONSOLIDATION.
 a. "A" Company will construct a "STRONG POINT" at S.E. corner of the POMMERN REDOUBT to protect the right flank. The garrison will be at least 1 Platoon.
 b. "B" Company will construct and occupy the "STRONG POINT" on spur between POMMERN REDOUBT and GALLIPOLI with 1 Platoon, 2 Lewis Guns and 2 Machine Guns. Observation etc as per last sub-para in para 13 of Brigade Operation Order No. 125.
(See 165 Infantry Brigade Operation Order No. 125 para 13)

※ at D.19.b.00.70 commanding ground to North & North East

9. STRONG POINT. constructed by the R.E's at about D.19.c.05.60 will be garrisoned by ½ a Platoon and 1 Lewis Gun of "C" Company on receipt of orders from Battalion Headquarters.

10. S.O.S. SIGNAL.
S.O.S. Signal will be the Rifle Grenade pattern bursting into two red and two green. These signals will be carried by Officers.

11. FLARES.
Flares will be lit behind cover or at the bottom of a trench when possible. They will only be lit by men in the most advanced position reached. They must on no account be lit by men behind. The signal for lighting the flares will be a white very light fired from an aeroplane. This will probably be preceded by a KLAXON HORN to draw attention to the aeroplane. WATSON FANS will also be issued for Signalling to aeroplanes.

12. PROTECTION OF FLANKS.
(See 165 Infantry Brigade Operation Order No. 125 para 17)
"C" Company will establish a defensive flank along CAMEL AVENUE from the "BLUE LINE" to the Road running from FREZENBERG past SQUARE FARM. The attention of "A" Company is drawn to SMOKE BARRAGE.

13. PRISONERS.
The Instructions contained in para 18 of 165 Infantry Brigade Operation Order No. 125 will be strictly adhered to as regards Prisoners.

14. CARE OF MEN.
It is of the utmost importance that men should get as much rest as possible. All men not actually required to work should be allotted dugouts when available and be allowed to rest undisturbed.

15. DRESS. (See Appendix 1)

16. COMMUNICATION.
Communication will be maintained until a cable is laid forward to Companies, by runner.
Posts are being established at UHLAN FARM, PLUM FARM, POMMERN CASTLE.
Special instructions have been issued to the Battalion Signalling Officer.
(See also 165th Infantry Brigade Operation Order No. 125 para 21)

17. REPORTS.
After the capture of an objective reports are required on the following points when applicable:-
Exact position, and if in touch with troops on flank. Condition of trench. Amount of cover etc - Action and position of neighbouring troops - position of hostile barrage - condition of C.T's - number and position of dugouts and accommodation, and whether shell proof - approximate casualties - prisoners or captured machine guns.

18. LIAISON.
O.C. "A" Company will establish Liaison Posts at C.30.b.60.95 and D.19.c.70.75 with 10/11th Battalion H.L.I. "B" and "D" Companies will also maintain touch with 9th King's on the left.

19. PACK ANIMALS.
Pack animals will be utilised to send up S.A.A. Bombs etc as soon as the "BLACK LINE" is captured.

20. TRAFFIC and POSTS.
After ZERO the STRAND will be an up Trench and BACOM a "DOWN" Trench. If the enemy's artillery fire is not heavy all movement after ZERO will be over the top. The following Straggler Posts will be established.

-4-

20. TRAFFIC and POSTS (Contd.).

    a. Junction of OXFORD TRENCH and STRAND.
    b. Junction of OXFORD TRENCH and PAGODA TRENCH.
    c. Junction of OXFORD TRENCH and LONE TRENCH.

(a) Posts will be found by the 5th King's, (b and c) by 6th King's. Posts will consist of 1 N.C.O. and 2 men. Posts a and b will also watch tracks No. 4 and 5 respectively. No unwounded man is to be allowed to pass these posts except runners and stretcher bearers. Men suffering from shell shock or gas will not be allowed to pass. All unauthorised men trying to pass these posts will have their names taken and will then be collected in OXFORD TRENCH near the STRAND. They will be available for carrying parties. Divisional Brigade Posts will be established at I.4.b.25.70. and I.4.a.42.85., each post consisting of 2 Regimental Police of 7th King's. Instructions have been issued by the Division to these posts.

21. DUMPS.

The following Battalion Dump has been established by the Brigade at the Junction of OXFORD TRENCH and STRAND, and contains S.A.A. Bombs, Water, R.E. material, etc. This will be in charge of Sgt. Edwards and 2 men.

22. SALVAGE.

No damage is to be done to captured guns or machine guns unless there appears to be a likelihood of their re-capture by the enemy. All captured rations, water tins, bombs and R.E. material will be collected in dumps and issued to troops as required under Battalion arrangements. All papers, maps, etc., which may be found in dugouts or on German Officers will be collected and sent to Battalion Headquarters. All maps and photos will be collected from our own casualties when possible and sent to Battalion Headquarters for re-distribution.

23. MEDICAL. (See Appendix 2).

24. WATER, TEA, etc. (See Appendix 3).

25. SURPLUS KIT. (See Appendix 4).

26. MAPS.

All Officers in the Attack will carry the following maps and message forms:-
    a. ST. JULIEN 1/10,000 ordinary trench map.
        ZONNEBEKE   "   "
        WESTROOSEBEKE   "   "
    b. FREZENBERG 1/10,000 brief size trench map.
    c. BARRAGE MAP - showing the movement of the barrage, Strong Points, supporting Points, liaison points etc.
    d. An adequate number of message forms with map on the back.

The above will be issued late.

27. ZERO HOUR will be notified later.

        A C K N O W L E D G E.

                                         Capt;
Adjt; 1/7th Bn "The King's" (L'pool Regt). T.F.

APPENDIX 1

DRESS:-

Fighting Order, with Packs instead of haversacks.

The following Bombs, Flares etc will be carried:-

LEWIS GUNNERS:-
    1 extra Iron Ration.
    3 Sandbags.
    2 Mill's Bombs.
    1 Water Bottle containing Tea.

BOMBERS:-
    12 Mills Bombs.
    1 extra Iron Ration.
    3 Sandbags.
    1 water bottle containing Tea.

RIFLE BOMBERS:-
    6 No 23's or No 24's Rifle Bombs.
    The men carrying Grenade Rifles will carry No 24's and the remainder of the Team No. 23's
    3 Sandbags
    2 Bombs.
    1 extra Iron Ration
    1 extra Water Bottle containing Tea

RIFLEMEN:-
    3 Sandbags.
    2 Mills Bombs.
    1 extra Iron Ration.
    1 extra Water Bottle

No. 2 Lewis Gunners will carry 4 magazines. Remaining magazines up to 30 will be distributed equally amongst the Platoon. The extra 14 magazines per gun will be stored at POTIJZE DUMP.

	"A"	"B"	"C"	"D"
Picks	15	15	15	15
Shovels	60	60	60	60
Smoke Bombs	25	25	-	10
S.O.S. Signals	10	10	-	5
Very Lights 1"	50	50	20	30
White Flares	100	100	-	50
S.O.S. Rifle Rockets	5	5	-	2
Smoke Candles	75	-	25	-

The S.O.S. Signals will be carried by Officers.

APPENDIX 2.

MEDICAL ARRANGEMENTS

(a) REGIMENTAL AID POSTS at ZERO:-
    C.28.d.6.7. (PAGODA STREET) for 2 attacking Battalions.
    Prior to assault the supporting Battalion will share these Aid Post.
    As advance progresses new Reg'l Aid Post will be selected by Units and the Advanced Dressing Station notified.

(b) COLLECTING POSTS, C.27.d.3.1. (JUNCTION ROAD)
    I.4.a.9.3. (POTIJZE)

(c) ADVANCED DRESSING STATION I.1.b.9.3. (Canal Bank)

Casualty List (Sheet 5)

MISSING.

269097	Pte	Franks J.S.	"A"	31-7-17	
268929	"	Leatherbarrow, J.R.	"A"	"	
265202	"	Walmsley F.J.	"A"	"	Now reported Wounded
269157	"	Low R.	"A"	"	" Adm 2/a Sick
~~267249~~	"	~~Wright R.~~	~~"A"~~	"	Rej'd Bn 5-8-17
265130	"	Gray, W.	"A"	"	
305021	"	Franks J	"A"	"	
266752	"	Clarke S.	"A"	"	
265838	"	Bond R.	"B"	"	
267828	"	Naylor H	"B"	"	
267360	"	Seymour W	"B"	"	
269394	"	Skinning J	"B"	"	
49855	"	Moss, J.W.	"B"	"	
268942	"	Thompson, J.	"B"	"	
269307	"	Boothman, G.	"C"	2-8-17	Now reported W. Bayonet (acc)
269018	"	Hardstaff, C	"C"	1-8-17	
267983	"	Pye W.H.	"C"	1-8-17	
267151	"	Baker, W.G.	"C"	2-8-17	
266923	"	Moore R.	"C"	1-8-17	
~~266663~~	"	~~Griffiths J~~	~~"C"~~	~~31-7-17~~	Rej'd Bn 5-8-17
265279	"	Poddy, C.J.	"D"	31-7-17	
269309	"	O'Kieff D	"B"	"	
266640	"	Burns E.C.	"B"	"	
268404	"	Langdon J.E.	"A"	"	Now reported Sick Adm 2/a
264024	"	Adcock J	"D"	"	" " to Burnell
269280	"	Reid R.	"B"	"	
266662	"	O'Reilly J	"B"	"	

APPENDIX 2 (Contd)

Any unwounded enemy that may be taken will be used to carry and help our wounded down to the Dressing Station. A reserve stretcher bearer will be earmarked in each Platoon to assist the wounded, if necessary, after all objectives have been gained.

All walking wounded will carry their arms and equipment and to be in charge of Prisoners (if any)

APPENDIX 3.

WATER, TEA etc.

The extra water bottle filled with tea on X Day will be carried in the Pack.

Breakfast will be made in the "Y" Day area late in the evening and carried up in Thermos Cans.

Water to fill No. 1 Water Bottle will be supplied from Water Cart on "Y" Day and night.

The Quartermaster will send Cocoa up with "Y" Day's rations.

The attention of all ranks is drawn to the necessity of returning empty Petrol Tins; unless this is done the supply of water cannot be guaranteed.

Narrative of Operations carried out by 1/7th Battalion "The King's" (Liverpool Regiment) T.F. on the 31st July 1917.

-o-o-o-o-o-o-o-o-o-o-o-o-o-o-o-

The Battalion formed up in 4 waves - the first wave between OXFORD TRENCH and WARWICK TRENCH, the second wave in OXFORD TRENCH, and the third and fourth waves each 100 Yards in rear of this trench. All ranks immediately dug-in.

The Battalion was in position at 11.30 p.m. 30.7.17.
Hot cocoa and rum were served at 2.30 a.m. 31.7.17.

At ZERO plus 30 minutes i.e. at 4.20 a.m. the Battalion left the assembly trenches.

Formation:-   "A" Company in 2 waves on Right.
             "D" Company in 2 waves on Left.
             "C" Company with 3 Platoons as moppers up for
                PLUM REDOUBT with first waves of leading Coys,
                1 Platoon with 3rd and 4th waves on Right.
             "B" Company in 3rd and 4th waves on Left.

'No mans land' was crossed with scarcely any casualties, enemy barrage being slight.

The crossing of the German Front Line System was difficult owing to the result of our bombardment, which had broken up the ground, and some of the enemy had to be accounted for who had been overlooked by leading Battalions.

The Battalion formed up on the BLUE LINE and waited for the barrage to lift.
At 5.15 a.m. the advance was commenced from the BLUE LINE.
The Right Company ("A") was held up by party of enemy and M.G. in SQUARE FARM which was dealt with effectively and the Right continued the Advance.
"C" Company Moppers up meanwhile had occupied PLUM REDOUBT and took up positions, 2 Platoons on line SQUARE FARM - PLUM FARM, 1 Platoon in reserve for R.E. Strong Point, and 1 Platoon formed defensive flank in CAMEL AVENUE.
On the left "B" Company, after passing through heavy shell and M.G. fire, crossed the Beke by bridges and entered POMMERN CASTLE on either flank at 6.5 a.m. Pigeon message was sent off at once.
The dugouts and trenches were mopped up and connection obtained with 9th Kings on Left and 15th Division on Right who were some way back to the Right rear. A Party under 2/Lieut. Leach was pushed out to construct a Strong Point on Hill 35 and came under severe M.G.Fire. The Strong Point was established on the N.W. side of the ridge. A light Field Gun was captured enroute to the position on Hill 35 and enemy were caught by Lewis Gun Fire when retiring.
The remainder of "B" Company proceeded to consolidate the position in POMMERN CASTLE, Captain Heaton taking up his main position on the West side of the Castle and when "A" Company arrived followed by "D" Company * he took command of the whole force and was untiring in the work of strengthening and consolidating the position.
Two Supporting Points were pushed out about 150 Yards to East of main defensive position and occupied at night. By day; an advance post was maintained at S.E.point of POMMERN CASTLE with telephonic communication to main trench.
"A" Company on the Right were held up at about 400 yards from their objective by enfilade M.G.Fire. A Tank that was operating about 600 Yards to the left came along on receipt of a message (gallantly taken by Pte Shaw) and enabled the Company to proceed and gain its objective at 9.30 a.m. The trenches were cleared of the enemy, when it was noticed that some of the enemy were manning some trenches in advance of the captured position. A party went forward and 3 Officers and 30 men were taken prisoners and this advanced position held. The work of consolidation was pushed on.

* only 1 junior Officer being left with A + D Coys.

- 2 -

Connection by means of a patrol was established with the Right Flank and when later on "C" Company from line SQUARE FARM - PLUM FARM came as reinforcxxxxements, the Line was completed to Right Div. "C" Company was ordered to reinforce the Front Line at 11.20 a.m. and a Company of 5th King's took over the line SQUARE- PLUM FARM.

"D" Company seemed to have gone too much to its Left, but 1 Platoon arrived in POMMERN CASTLE with "B" Company and shared the task of clearing up the place and consolidating. Later on, at about 9 a.m. the other part of "D" Company arrived at its objective which had already been dealt with.

About 10 a.m. the 164 Brigade passed through our position, and were assisted by fire of our M.G's and Lewis Guns, especially from Strong Point at Hill 35. This Strong Point was compelled later to withdraw its garrison the Machine Guns and Lewis Gun having been knocked out.
When the 164 Brigade fell back at 5.20 p.m. special measures were taken to secure the position. Lewis Guns were pushed out to the front and Machine Guns arranged to cover the front. Some men of this Brigade stayed in POMMERN CASTLE but were ordered to withdraw at midnight.

Enemy were seen massing during the course of the afternoon but their counter-attack on this day failed to develop, being broken up by artillery fire. In this connection our rifles and Lewis Gun fire played effectively on groups of the enemy seen massing in the vicinity of IBERIAN.

Battalion Headquarters was established at UHLAN FARM at 5 a.m. and moved up to POMMERN CASTLE on receipt of Brigade instructions to do so.

Line Held and consolidated:-
 D.19.c.75.80 to D.19.a.67.02 thence along Southern portion of POMMERN REDOUBT to D.19.a.10.30.

Comdg.1/7th Bn. "The King's" (Liverpool Regiment) Lieut.Col., T.F.

9th August 1917.

WAR DIARY of **INTELLIGENCE SUMMARY**

Army Form C. 2118.

1st SHEET.

(Erase heading not required.) 7th KING'S (LPOOL) REGT.

Instructions regarding War Diaries and Intelligence Summaries are contained in F. S. Regs., Part II. and the Staff Manual respectively. Title Pages will be prepared in manuscript.

Place	Date	Hour	Summary of Events and Information	Remarks and references to Appendices
Trenches	April 1916. 1st		Relieved in Trenches by 9th Kings & proceeded to Billets in BEAUMETZ	
BEAUMETZ	2 "		Church Parade.	
"	3 "		Bathing huts and Working Parties.	
"	4 "		" " "	
"	5 "		Working Parties.	
"	6 "		Working Parties. Corps Commander inspected 1 Coy & expressed himself very pleased with the Kings Appearance	
"	7 "		Relieved the 9th Kings in the Trenches	
TRENCHES	8 "		Trench Routine nothing unusual	
"	9 "		" " " "	
"	10 "		" " " "	
"	11 "		" " " "	
"	12 "		" " " "	
"	13 "		" " " " Relieved in Front Line by 9th Kings	
MAILLY	14 "		cleaning up and Working Parties.	
"	15 "		Bathing huts Working Parties	
"	16 "		Divine Service and Working parties	
"	17 "		" " Working parties	
"	18 "		Working Parties	
"	19 "		Relieved the 9th Kings in front trenches	
TRENCHES	20 "		usual Trench Routine nothing unusual	
"	21 "		" " " "	
"	22 "		" " " "	
"	23 "		" " " "	
"	24 "		" " " "	
"	25 "		As relieved by 9th Kings & proceeded to Billets in BEAUMETZ	

Army Form C. 2118.

WAR DIARY
or
INTELLIGENCE SUMMARY

(Erase heading not required.) 7th KING'S (LIVERPOOL) R.T. & I.

2nd Sheet

Place	Date	Hour	Summary of Events and Information	Remarks and references to Appendices
FLETRES BEAUMETZ	April 26th		Cleaning of Clothing and Equipment	
—	27.		Coy Parades and inspection, and specialist classes	
—	28.		" " "	
—	29.		" " "	
—	30.		Church Parades	

Edward [signature]
Lieut-Colonel,
Commanding 13th King's (Liverpool) Regt.

April 1918
War Diary
for
7th Bn. Kings (Liverpool R)

Army Form C. 2118.

WAR DIARY
or
INTELLIGENCE SUMMARY
(Erase heading not required.)

1st Sheet. 7th King's L'pool Regt.

Place	Date	Hour	Summary of Events and Information	Remarks and references to Appendices
	MAY 1916			
WAILLY	1.		Relieved 9th Kings in front line Trenches	
TRENCHES	2.		Usual trench routine	
"	3.		" " "	
"	4.		" " "	
"	5.		" " "	
"	6.		" " "	
"	7.		" " "	
"	8.		Relieved by 9th Kings and billeted in WAILLY	
WAILLY	9.			
"	10.		Usual working parties & cleaning the village	
"	11.			
"	12.			
"	13.		Divine service and working parties	
"	14.		Relieved 9th Kings in front line Trenches	
TRENCHES	15.			
"	16.		Usual Trench Routine	
"	17.			
"	18.			
"	19.			
"	20.		Relieved by 9th Kings. Battalion proceeded to Beaumetz in billets	
"	21.			

11c

7th Batn "King's" (L'pool Regt)
War Diary for May

Army Form C. 2118.

WAR DIARY
or
INTELLIGENCE SUMMARY

(Erase heading not required.)

2nd Sheet 1/7th KING'S Lpool REGT. Vol 15

Place	Date	Hour	Summary of Events and Information	Remarks and references to Appendices
BEAUMETZ	May 1916 22.		General cleaning up and Coy inspection	
"	23.		Coy parades, working parties at night.	
"	24.		"	
"	25.		Adjutant's Parade, and Coy parades working parties.	
"	26.		"	
"	27.		"	
"	28.		"	
TRENCHES	29.		Divine service in the morning, at 12 noon inspection by C.O. Visit who complimented the Battalion on its excellent turnout and appearance. Relieved 9 the King's in front line trenches at 11pm.	
"	30.		10 Additional Officers joined for duty.	
"	31.		Usual Trench Routine	

Seymour ?
Lieut-Colonel
Commanding 1/7th King's

Army Form C. 2118.

165/55

1st Sheet.   7th King's (Liverpool Regt)   Vol 16

WAR DIARY
INTELLIGENCE SUMMARY
(Erase heading not required.)

Place	Date 1916	Hour	Summary of Events and Information	Remarks and references to Appendices
TRENCHES	June 1		Usual Trench routine	
"	2		" " "	
"	3		" " "	
"	4		Relieved by 9th King's. Billets in Wailly	
WAILLY	5		Working parties and cleaning of munitions	
"	6		" " "	
"	7		" " "	
"	8		" " "	
"	9		" " "	
"	10		" " "	
"	11		Divine service and working parties	
"	12		Working parties. Relieved 9th King's in trenches	
TRENCHES	13		Usual Trench routine	
"	14		" " "	
"	15		" " "	
"	16		" " "	
"	17		" " "	
"	18		" " "	
"	19		" " "	
"	20		" " "	
"	21		" " "	
"	22		" " "	
"	23		" " "	
"	24		" " "	
"	25		" " "	
"	26		Relieved by 14th R. Fusiliers 5th A.D. Battalion to Billets in BEAUMETZ	
"	27		Cleaning up clothing & equipment	
"	28		Working parties. Battalion moved to Bivouacs in Gouy-Rein in September Infantry Special School	
"	29		" " in training	
"	30		" " "	

Signed,
Lt-Colonel
Commanding 7th King's (Liverpool Regt)

12e

June 1916

Wm Drury

4th Bn. Kings
Liverpool Regt

55th Division

Vol 30

26e

War Diary
of
1/7th Liverpool R.
for period
1st to 31st August. 1917.

Army Form C. 2118.

WAR DIARY
or
INTELLIGENCE SUMMARY

(Erase heading not required.) 1/4 Bn The KING'S (LPOOL REGT.) T.F.

SHEET. I.

Place	Date	Hour	Summary of Events and Information	Remarks and references to Appendices
	Aug 1917			
POMMERN.	1.		} Consolidation and holding the position taken on the 31-7-17.	
"	2.			
"	3.		Relieved by a Bn. of R. W. Surreys in the morning. Bn moved to vicinity POTIJZE & later in the day to VLAMERTINGHE thence by Bus to HILLHOEK. P.15.	
HILHOEK	4.		} Cleaning up, refitting	
"	5.			
"	6.		Moved to LOUCHES by Rail and Motor Lorries.	
LOUCHES	7 to 31.		} Refitting and training	

C.H. Potts. Lieut-Colonel.
Comdg. 1/4 Bn The King's (Lpool Regt) T.F.

CONFIDENTIAL

WD 31

War Diary

of

1/7 Liverpool R

For Period

1/9/17 – 30/9/17

27e

Army Form C. 2118.

WAR DIARY
or
INTELLIGENCE SUMMARY.
(Erase heading not required.) 1/4th Bn. The Kings (Liverpool Regt) T.F.

Place	Date	Hour	Summary of Events and Information	Remarks and references to Appendices
September 1919				
Reverts	1st to 14th		Training	
"	15th		Moved via RUDRUISE to VLAMERTINGHE No 2 Area	
No 2 Area	16		Settling down to the lines	
"	17		Moved forward to Old British Reserve Front-line System	
Trenches	18		Y.4th Bn. A + C received the 1/5 Stores in POPPEREN	
"	19		Y. DAY. Preparing to operations	
"	20		Z. " operations, Copy 1 opera. not received marked	
"	21		Z+1 day consolidation of taken	
"	22		Z+2 " " relieved by 2/5 S. Staffs Regt.	
"	23		Relief complete at 1.30 am Bn moved to No 2 Henninghe & marched in the afternoon to FORTH CAMP WATOU AREA	
FORTH CAMP	24		Resting	
"	25		"	
"	26		Marched to PESELHOEK entrained with Transport and moved to BRAUVE then marched to BRASTRE	

Army Form C. 2118.

WAR DIARY
or
INTELLIGENCE SUMMARY.
(Erase heading not required.) 1/7 Bn. The King's (Pool Regt) T.F.

2nd SHEET

Instructions regarding War Diaries and Intelligence Summaries are contained in F. S. Regs., Part II. and the Staff Manual respectively. Title pages will be prepared in manuscript.

Place	Date 1917	Hour	Summary of Events and Information	Remarks and references to Appendices
BARASTRE	September 27		Training and reorganising	
"	28		"	
"	29		"	
"	30		"	
			Casualties during operations 20th to 23rd Sept 1917	
	Officers			
	Killed		Captain R Shout. Lieuts S.F. Vick & S.H. Heatersmith	
	Died of Wounds		2nd Lts M Dresson & A.F. O'Neill	
	Wounded		Lieuts J.D. Johnson, R.R. Robinson E.S. Clay, F. Killyon	
	O. Ranks			
	Killed		61.	
	Wounded		166	
	Missing		12	
	Died of Wounds		3	
	Total		242	

C.H. Potter. Lieut-Colonel.
Comdg 1/7 Bn. The King's (Lpool Regt) T.F.

1/7 Bn The Kings (L'pool Regt)

1/7th BN. "THE KING'S" (LIVERPOOL REGIMENT) T.F.

NARRATIVE of OPERATIONS from 20th to 22nd SEPTEMBER, 1917, inclusive.

Box 4927

"Z" DAY.

ASSEMBLY. The Assembly position of the Battalion was a line of shell holes and disused trenches in front of POMMERN REDOUBT. This line was taped out on Y/Z night and the Battalion was in position at 4.0 a.m. and in touch on the right with the South African Brigade and on the left with the 9th King's.

DISPOSITIONS. The Battalion formed up in four waves as follows:-

——————————— Enemy. ———————————

"C" Company.   ↑   "B" Company.

"D" Company.   "A" Company.

The right flank of the Battalion being on the ZONNEBEKE.

OBJECTIVES. Two objectives were allotted to the Battalion:-
(1) A line running through IBERIAN FARM, IRMA FARM, KAYNORTH to ZONNEBEKE.
(2) A line running approximately North and South of DELVA FARM.

The two leading Companies ("B" and "C") were to go to the 2nd Objective; the two rear Companies ("A" and "D") to the 1st Objective.

Platoons specially detailed for Strong Points were as follows:-
    No. 14 Platoon   IBERIAN FARM.
    " 13   "   IRMA FARM.
    "   1   "   KAYNORTH.
    " 11   "   DELVA FARM.

ATTACK. The line of attack was due East and ix along the bank of the ZONNEBEKE.
At ZERO the first lines advanced and got close under the barrage, followed by the rear waves. Almost immediately on leaving the assembly position the Battalion suffered casualties from Machine Guns at KAYNORTH, IBERIAN FARM and HILL 35. The ground was literally a mass of shell holes and got worse as progress was made. This casued the lines and waves to become mixed up.
The first waves were held up by the Strong Points IBERIAN FARM and KAYNORTH, which comprised a number of reinforced concrete dugouts. The supporting waves pushed on and reinforced. The platoons detailed to take the Strong Points failed on account of heavy cross Machine Gun fire. On account of its being on high ground, the most bitter fighting was round IBERIAN FARM. Several gallant attempts to rush the Point failed. It was finally stormed at 6.45 a.m. with the assistance of Machine Guns, Lewis Guns, Rifle Grenades and Bombs. KAYNORTH was captured about the same time with the assistance of the South Africans on the right flank.

CAPTURE of OBJECTIVES. At 7.0 a.m. the 1st Objective was in our hands and consolidation commenced. Meanwhile, parties were re-organised and advanced on the 2nd Objective. The only opposition to be met with was from snipers in shell holes and Machine Gun fire from HILL 37. The 2nd Objective was captured at 8.30 a.m. Two Strong Points were constructed, one at DELVA FARM and the other between DELVA FARM and the ZONNEBEKE.

"Z" DAY (contd).

CONSOLIDATION. Five Strong Points were constructed on the 1st Objective line; two on the second objective line.

COUNTER ATTACK. About 5-30 p.m. the enemy bombarded our position and a counter attack was expected. It did not however, develope on our front.

"Z" plus 1 DAY.

At 4-30 a.m. the enemy placed a heavy barrage on our Lines until daybreak. The day was quiet expect for intervals of shelling. Enemy aeroplanes were active over our new position.
At 5 p.m. a very heavy bombardment commenced which did not cease until 8-15 p.m. No counter attack developed on our front. We only suffered three casualties from this shelling.

"Z" plus 2 DAY.

At dawn and dusk the enemy placed a barrage on our lines. There was heavy shelling at intervals during the day.
The 2/5th S. Staff; Regt arrived in the Trenches about 9 p.m. to relieve the Battalion.

"Z" plus 3 DAY.

1.30 a.m. Relief complete.

C.H. Potter. Lieut-Col;
Comdg, 1/7th Bn "The King's" (Liverpool Regt).

25-9-17

CONFIDENTIAL

% 32

28c

War Diary
of
1/7th Liverpool C.R.
for the period
1st to 31st October, 1917

SECRET

Army Form C. 2118.

WAR DIARY
or
INTELLIGENCE SUMMARY.

(Erase heading not required.) 1/1 Bⁿ "The King's" (L'pool Regt)

Instructions regarding War Diaries and Intelligence Summaries are contained in F. S. Regs., Part II. and the Staff Manual respectively. Title pages will be prepared in manuscript.

of 1st King's

Place	Date	Hour	Summary of Events and Information	Remarks and references to Appendices
	OCTOBER			
TIZECOURT LE-BAS.	1st	—	In Camp	
TRENCHES	2nd	—	Moved via ST EMELIE into support, LEMPIRE.	
"	6th		Relieved the 5th Kings in the Right Section (BILLEMONT FARM)	
"	12th		Relieved by 1/4 Kings Own and moved into Support, LEFT Section - VAUGHAN BANK, MEATH POST, 14 WILLOWS LANE, and LIMERICK POST	
"	17th		Relieved 9th Kings in Centre Section Left Brigade Front	
"	23		Relieved by 10th Inniskillings and moved to billets in LONGAVESNES	
LONGAVESNES	23 to 31		} Cleaning, etc.	

C.B. Ritter Lieut Col
Comdg. 1/1 Bⁿ The King's (L'pool Regt)

165/55 9/11 33

War Diary
of the
11th Liverpool R
1st Welsh Regiment
1st to 31st November
1917

Army Form C. 2118.

WAR DIARY
INTELLIGENCE SUMMARY
(Erase heading not required.)

1ST SHEET   1/7TH BN. KING'S (LIVERPOOL REGT.) T.F.

Place	Date	Hour	Summary of Events and Information	Remarks and references to Appendices
	NOVEMBER 1917			
LONGAESNES	1		Training	
"	3		Moved to Trenches. Relieved 1/8 Shrop. Centre Sector Right Brigade	
Trenches	3 to 15		Trench Routine	
	16		Relieved 1/8 Irish. Moved to VILLERS-FAUCON	
VILLERS FAUCON	17		Moved to TINCOURT	
TINCOURT	18		Inspection. Relieving Bn.	
	19		Moved to LEMPIRE as support Bn.	
LEMPIRE	20		In support. British attack Commenced	
"	21		In support	
"	22		Relieved 4/1 K. Rifles in GILLEMONT Sector	
"	23 to 29		Trench Routine	
Trenches	30		Enemy attack on our Right. Counter attack on our Left. Counter attack...	C.R.H. Crady Lieut Colonel Comdg 1/7 For The King's (Liverpool Regt) T.F.

Secret & Confidential

War Diary
for
the month of
December 1917.

1/7th Bn "The King's" (L'pool Regt)

WAR DIARY
or
INTELLIGENCE SUMMARY.

Army Form C. 2118.

1st SHEET. 1/7th The King's (Loyal) Regt. T.F.

Place	Date	Hour	Summary of Events and Information	Remarks and references to Appendices
TRENCHES	Apr 1/17	10 AM	GILLEMONT FARM SECTOR.	
"		11 AM		
"		3 PM	Relieved by 10 R. Dublin Fusiliers. Moved to St Emilie.	
"		6 PM	Moved by Bus to PERONNE.	
ST EMILIE	6			
PERONNE	7		Billets. Resting	
"	8		Moved from PERONNE to MARQUIL Y.Camp	
MARQUIL	9		Training	
"	10 11		"	
"	12		Moved by March Route to TINQUES	
TINQUES	13		" " " BOLAS	
BOLAS	14		" " " CRÉPY	
CRÉPY	15 to 31		Training	

O/R the Lieut-Colonel
Comdg 1/7th The King's
(Loyal Regt) T.F.

CONFIDENTIAL

Vol 35

31e

War Diary
of
1/7th Liverpool R.
for the period
1st to 31st January 1918

Army Form C. 2118.

WAR DIARY
or
INTELLIGENCE SUMMARY.
(Erase heading not required.)

of SHEET 1/7 K.BN THE KING'S (Liverpool Regt.) T.F.

Place	Date	Hour	Summary of Events and Information	Remarks and references to Appendices
CREPY	1st to 31st		Training. Draft of 5 Officers and 137 O.Rs. from 1/8th Bn. The King's (Liverpool Regt) T.F. joined on the 31st January 1918.	

R. Arthur Lt-Colonel
Comdg 1/7 Bn. The King's (Liverpool Regt.) T.F.

Vol 36

32e

War Diary
of the
1/7th Liverpools
for the period
1st to 28th Febry
1918.

Army Form C. 2118.

WAR DIARY
or
INTELLIGENCE SUMMARY.
(Erase heading not required.)

Instructions regarding War Diaries and Intelligence Summaries are contained in F. S. Regs., Part II. and the Staff Manual respectively. Title pages will be prepared in manuscript.

Place	Date	Hour	Summary of Events and Information	Remarks and references to Appendices
CREPY	1-2-18 to 4-2-18		Training	
CREPY	8-2-18		Moved by route march to LIGNY-LEZ-AIRE.	
LIGNY LEZ AIRE	9-2-18		Marched to L'ECLEME.	
L'ECLEME	10-2-18		Resting.	
"	11th		Bn. Bathing.	
"	12th		Marched to FERME DU ROI.	
FERME DU ROI	13th		Relieved 1/1 E. Lancs. (42nd Divn.) Support Bn. Hdqrs at WINDY CORNER.	
WINDY CORNER	14th - 18th		Working parties & usual routine.	
"	19th		Relieved 6th King's Liv'pool Rgt in Right Subsection, GIVENCHY Sector.	
TRENCHES	20th - 24th		Usual routine.	
"	25th		Relieved by 10th L'pool Scottish and moved to LE PREOL.	
LE PREOL	26th - 28th		Training and Working Parties	

Arthur Rh. Lt Col.
Comdg. 1/7 Bn. "The King's" L'pool Regt.

Vol 37

War
Diary
of
117th Liverpool R
for
1st to 31st March
1918

Army Form C. 2118.

WAR DIARY
or
INTELLIGENCE SUMMARY.
(Erase heading not required.)

1/4th Batt. The King's (Kent Regt.?) 1st Sheet

Place	Date	Hour	Summary of Events and Information	Remarks and references to Appendices
	March 1915			
EPREOL	1st		Battalion in Divisional Reserve	
"	2		"	
"	3		"	
"	4 to 8		Relieved 4/4th Scottish in GIVENCHY SECTOR left Sub-Sector.	
Trenches			Holding Trenches	
"	9		Relieved in Trenches by 4/5 King's (Liverpool Regt) 2 Coys to GORRE	
FME-DU-ROI & GORRE	10		FME-DU-ROI 2 Coys to GORRE	
"	11 – 13		Support Bttalion in Brigade Reserve	
"	14		Relieved 4/5 King's (Liverpool Regt) in GIVENCHY Right Sub-Sector	
TRENCHES	15		Trench Routine	
"	16		"	
"	17		by 4th money	
"	17 to 27		Relieved 1/5 LANCS to FESTUBERT Secn Regt Sub-Sector relieving 4/5 Scot Trench Routine	
"	27		Relieved by 1/6 Kings. Battalion moved to GORRE	

P.T.O.

WAR DIARY
or
INTELLIGENCE SUMMARY.
(Erase heading not required.)

2nd Sheet. 1/7th Bn THE KING'S (Liverpool REGT) T.F.

Army Form C. 2118.

Place	Date	Hour	Summary of Events and Information	Remarks and references to Appendices
	March 1918			
GORRE	28		Support Battalion in Brigade Reserve	
"	29		" " "	
"	30		" " "	
Tuneles	31		Relieved 1/5th Kings (Liverpool Regt) in FESTUBERT Sector Right Sub Sector	

CR Pitter. Lieut-Colonel.
Commanding 1/7th Bn The King's (Liverpool Regt) T.F.

165th Brigade.

55th Division.

1/7th BATTALION

THE KING'S LIVERPOOL REGIMENT

APRIL 1918.

M 38

16/5

War Diary
of
17 Knockworth
1st personal
1st to 30th April
1918

SECRET

WAR DIARY
or
INTELLIGENCE SUMMARY.
(Erase heading not required.)

Army Form C. 2118.

Place	Date April	Hour	Summary of Events and Information	Remarks and references to Appendices
TRENCHES	1-3rd		In FESTUBERT Sector. Regtl Instr acting.	
"	4th		GERMAN attack. Nothing attracted	
"	14th	1-20am	Relieved by 1/6th Devon (Spear Reg) and marched to TUNING FORK AREA	
"	15th		Relieved by 1st Nulm Borderers 1st Division and moved by Bus to AUCHEL arriving AUCHEL Apr 16th.	
AUCHEL	23rd		moved to VERQUIN	
VERQUIN	24th		moved to LABOURSE	
LABOURSE	27th		moved into support line LE PREOL relieving the 1/10th (Garnets) 1st Devon (Spear Reg)	
TRENCHES	29th		Relieved 1/5th Bn Devon (Spear Reg) in FESTUBERT Sector. Left Instr acting.	
"	30th		In FESTUBERT Sector. Left Instr acting.	

C.B.Potter Lieut Col
Comdg 1/7 Bn Hastings (Spear Reg)

1/7th Battalion, "The King's" (Liverpool Regiment)

NARRATIVE OF OPERATIONS 9th April to 15th April 1918.
-o-o-o-o-o-o-o-o-o-

The Battalion relieved the 5th K.L.R. in the FESTUBERT SOUTH Sector on the evening of the 31st March 1918, and took up the following dispositions:-

RIGHT FRONT COMPANY:-
    1 Platoon   PRINCE'S ISLAND.
    1   "   GEORGE STREET.
    2 Platoons   OLD BRITISH LINE, astride CHESHIRE ROAD.

LEFT FRONT COMPANY:-
    1 Platoon   BARNTON TRENCH.
    1   "   BARNTON TEE.
    2 Platoons   OLD BRITISH LINE, astride BARNTON ROAD.

RIGHT SUPPORT COMPANY:-   VILLAGE LINE.
    2 Platoons   LE PLANTIN SOUTH
    2   "   CHESHIRE ROAD defences.

LEFT SUPPORT COMPANY:-   VILLAGE LINE.
    3 Platoons   LE PLANTIN NORTH
    1 Platoon   CONVENT Defences.

The situation from 31st March to 6th April was suspiciously quiet, but on the nights 6th, 7th and 8th extraordinary movement was heard in rear of enemy's line. On the 5th inst 1 Company of the Supporting Battalion was brought up to the VILLAGE LINE, 3 Platoons being in dugouts in VILLAGE LINE and 1 Platoon in TRAMWAYS HOUSE.

OPERATIONS:-

At 4-10 a.m. 9th April 1918, the enemy opened an intense gas bombardment all along the various lines which continued until 8 a.m., when it was noticed that gas shells were no longer being sent over, but the the H.E. bombardment had if anything, increased. There was a heavy ground mist which made observation impossible.

At 9-10 a.m. a runner came down from PRINCE'S ISLAND with a verbal message, saying that the enemy were attacking, a similar message coming from the left Front Company. The garrisons of these trenches were overpowered, as also were those of GEORGE STREET and BARNTON TEE, the enemy coming in from each flank and taking the position from the rear, only 5 men from GEORGE STREET being able to get back to the O.B. LINE.

About 9-50 a.m. the enemy advanced on the O.B. LINE attacking both from the front and on each flank, the garrison again being surprised. The Company Commanders then ordered the remainder of their Companies to withdraw to the VILLAGE LINE. This was done slowly, a rearguard being formed and the enemy kept back, "A" Coy. working down YELLOW ROAD and "D" Coy. down BARNTON TRENCH. By this time the barrage had lifted from the VILLAGE LINE and it was possible to organise the defence of same, "A" Coy. being placed in position astride YELLOW ROAD and "D" Coy. in the CONVENT and BARNTON ROAD Defences.

About 12 noon it was obvious the enemy were advancing in force on the VILLAGE LINE, rapid rifle and M.G. fire being opened, and through the mist large parties of the enemy could be seen in front of YELLOW ROAD and LE PLANTIN SOUTH, endeavouring to get through our wire. Cries of CEASE FIRE from the Germans spurred the garrisons to increase their volume of fire, and it could then be seen that, as far as a frontal attack was concerned there was nothing to fear.

Very few of the enemy approached the lines in front of LE PLANTIN NORTH, all that did so were shot down.

The supporting Platoon of 6th K.L.R. arrived about 12 noon and reinforced the garrison of LE PLANTIN NORTH, Captain McLaren taking command of the position.

Meantime patrols sent out from LE PLANTIN LE PLANTIN SOUTH to get in touch on the right had failed to return and at 12.30 p.m. it was reported that enemy had broken through between LE PLANTIN SOUTH and WINDY CORNER and were working round in rear of the former position. A bombing post formed on the right was rushed by the enemy and immediately afterwards, under cover of a T.M. bombardment, at least 200 Germans rushed the position and forced the garrison to withdraw Northwards where a position was established astride the road forming a defensive flank on the right of CHESHIRE ROAD Defences.

Meanwhile Headquarters Details, including Cooks, spare Signallers, Pioneers, etc., had been ordered to take up a position in A.7.b. behind some old breastworks in order to stop the enemy rolling up the VILLAGE LINE, and 2 Platoons of 6th K.L.R. coming up in support were quickly got in position facing South joining up VILLAGE LINE from Northern point of LE PLANTIN SOUTH to the old breastworks on Route 20, a defensive flank from SOUTH and WEST being formed. This manoevre appeared to defeat the enemy who were forced to withdraw towards the LA BASSEE CANAL.

About the same time the enemy attacked the BARNTON locality but were driven off leaving prisoners in our hands.

As there was very little activity in the centre of my position, I withdrew a portion of my garrison and sent them to replace a portion of the LE PLANTIN SOUTH garrison whom I ordered to retake the lost position. Captain J.W. Cook, M.C., commanding the garrison had meantime organised an attack assisted by Captain M.T. Leach, M.C., and had succeeded in capturing a portion of this position and the reinforcements having arrived the breastworks were quickly occupied. The enemy were found to be lying outside in large numbers, and on rapid fire being opened on them they retired in disorder, enormous casualties being inflicted; three captured German M.Gs were mounted on the parapet in addition which added greatly to the volume of fire. I then ordered the houses in the vicinity to be cleared. This work was very efficiently done headed by Captain Cook, and on reaching the southernmost house I ordered patrols to go forward to WINDY CORNER to clear up the situation. On return these patrols reported that the Lancashire Fusiliers were then in possession. I then ordered 2 Platoons, 6th K.L.R, who had been forming my right defensive flank, to swing round and take up a position on the VILLAGE ROAD, linking up LE PLANTIN SOUTH with WINDY CORNER. Patrols were then pushed out for the night and it was reported that the enemy were holding strong points at junctions of O.B. LINE and FIFE ROAD and BARNTON TRENCH.

On the morning of the 10th the enemy were seen to be massing in the O.B. LINE opposite LE PLANTIN NORTH. This concentration was effectively dealt with by artillery. An attempt to dislodge the enemy from his strong Point at junction of FIFE ROAD and O.B. LINE failed, and in order to safeguard the flank of the Battalion on my right, I established a post about A.2.d.65.10. In addition forward posts were established at junction of CHESHIRE ROAD and YELLOW ROAD; also in BARNTON ROAD about A.2.b.00.55.

On subsequent days the whole position was heavily bombarded with all calibre shells; also M.G. barrage was put down but no infantry action followed.

The Battalion less 1 Company was relieved on the 14th inst after being in the line for 15 days, the remaining Company being relieved on the night of the 15th on Divisional Relief.

16 German Machine Guns, 1 Flammenwerfer, and numerous signalling apparatus was captured in addition to about 200 prisoners, who however were not all passed through Brigade H.Q.

(Sd.) C.K. POTTER, Lieut. Col.
Comdg. 1/7th Bn. "The King's" (L'pool Regiment) T.F.

17.4.18.

WO 39

35-e

War Diary
of
11th Liverpool R
for period
1st to 31st May
1918.

Army Form C. 2118.

WAR DIARY
INTELLIGENCE SUMMARY.
(Erase heading not required.)

SECRET

MAY 1918

Place	Date	Hour	Summary of Events and Information	Remarks and references to Appendices
In the Field	MAY 1st		Battalion holding left sub section of FESTUBERT Sector (Sept Bde)	
"	2nd		Relieved and moved into support relieving 1/4 R. Lancs	
"	4th		5" Stays in Right sub section, GIVENCHY Section (Right Bde)	
"	8		Bn 1/4 N. Lancs and moved into Div reserve at VERQUENEUL	
"	14		1/5 Stays Own in support Section Sept Brigade	
"	16		6 Stays FESTUBERT Section left sub section	
"	20		Bn 1/10 Scottish and took over Support Section GIVENCHY	
"	22		6 Stays, Right sector, Sept sub section	
"	26		Bn 1/4 N. Lancs and moved into Div reserve 3 Coys to VERQUIN and 1 Coy to VERQUINEUL — Usual training carried out.	

C H Potter Lt Col
Comdg 1/7 R Lanc Regt

Vol 40

War Diary
of
1/7 Liverpool R
for
June 1918.

WAR DIARY
OR
INTELLIGENCE SUMMARY.

(Erase heading not required.)

Army Form C. 2118.

Instructions regarding War Diaries and Intelligence Summaries are contained in F. S. Regs., Part II. and the Staff Manual respectively. Title pages will be prepared in manuscript.

Place	Date	Hour	Summary of Events and Information	Remarks and references to Appendices
VAUDRICOURT	June 1		Bn. Divisional Reserve. Training	
"	2		Relieved 1/5th Bn South Lancashire Regt. in Left Subsector FESTUBERT SECTOR	
Trenches	4		Relieved in line by 1/5th Bn "The Kings" (Liverpool Regt) at and moved	
"			to SUPPORT - FESTUBERT SECTOR	
"	8		Relieved in Support by 1/5th Bn South Lancashire Regiment and	
"			took over Right Subsector GIVENCHY SECTOR from 2/5th Bn.	
"			Lancashire Fusiliers. Bn. H.Qrs. at VILLA GENIE	
"	11		Bn. H.Qrs move to FANSHAWE CASTLE	
"	14		Relieved in trenches by 1/4th Bn. Loyal North Lancs Regt. and	
"			moved into "BUSTLE" positions Bn. H.Qrs. LE PREOL Bivvys (near CANAL HOUSE)	
LE PREOL	15	5 am	"STAND DOWN" and moved to DROUVIN Camp. (A Bn Div Reserve)	
DROUVIN Camp	15/20		Bn Div Reserve training. (165 Bde Horse Show 19.6.18)	
"	20		Relieved 1/5th Bn "Kings Own" (R.L) Regt in SUPPORT, FESTUBERT SECTOR	
"	23		Relieved by 1/6th Bn "The Kings" (Liverpool Regt) S.S in Left Subsector FESTUBERT SECTOR	
Trenches	26		Relieved by 1/5th South Lancashire Regiment and moved into "BUSTLE" positions	
"	27		Relieved by 8/4th Bn "Kings Own" (Royal Lancs) Regt. in Left Subsector GIVENCHY Sector	
"	30		Relieved by 1/5 Bn "The Kings" (Liverpool Regt) S.S and moved into Support GIVENCHY SECTOR	

War Diary
of
117th Greenhow R
for period
1st to 31st July,
1918

Vol 41

37e.

SECRET & CONFIDENTIAL

Army Form C. 2118.

WAR DIARY
INTELLIGENCE SUMMARY
(Erase heading not required.)

JULY, 1918.

Instructions regarding War Diaries and Intelligence Summaries are contained in F.S. Regs., Part II. and the Staff Manual respectively. Title pages will be prepared in manuscript.

Place	Date July 1918	Hour	Summary of Events and Information	Remarks and references to Appendices
In the Field	1st-2nd		Battalion holding SUPPORT positions, GIVENCHY Sector.	
"	3rd		Relieved by 1/4th Bn. Loyal North Lancs Regt. and moved into "BUSTLE" positions.	
"	4th		Moved into Divisional Reserve at VAUDRICOURT.	
"	4th-6th		In Divisional Reserve. Usual training carried out.	
"	7th		Church Parades and Presentation of Ribands and Bars by G.O.C. Division for gallantry award worn by Officers and Other Ranks since January 1st 1918.	
"	8th-9th		Usual training carried out.	
"	9th		Relieved 1/10th (Scottish) Bn. "The King's" (Liverpool Regt.) in Right Sub-section, FESTUBERT Sector.	
"	15th		Relieved by 1/5th King's Own (Royal Lancaster) Regt and moved into "BUSTLE" positions.	
"	16th		Relieved 1/4th Bn. King's Own (Royal Lancaster) Regt. in Support positions, GIVENCHY Sector.	
"	19th		Relieved 1/6th Bn. "The King's" (Liverpool Regt) in left Sub-section, GIVENCHY Sector.	
"	22nd		Relieved by 1/4th Bn. King's Own (Royal Lancaster) Regt. and moved into "BUSTLE" positions.	
"	23rd		Moved into Divisional Reserve at VAUDRICOURT.	
"	23rd-28th		In Divisional Reserve. Usual training carried out.	
"	28th		Relieved 1/10th (Scottish) Bn. "The King's" (Liverpool Regt) in left Sub-section, FESTUBERT Sector.	
"	31st		Relieved by 1/5th Bn. "The King's" (Liverpool Regt) and moved into Support positions, FESTUBERT Sector.	

C.H. Potter
Comdg 1/7th Bn. The King's (Liverpool Regt.)

Vol 42

38e

War Diary
of
11th Liverpool R
1st to 31st August,
1918.

Army Form C. 2118.

WAR DIARY
INTELLIGENCE SUMMARY.
(Erase heading not required.)

Instructions regarding War Diaries and Intelligence Summaries are contained in F. S. Regs., Part II. and the Staff Manual respectively. Title pages will be prepared in manuscript.

Place	Date	Hour	Summary of Events and Information	Remarks and references to Appendices
Trenches	August 1918 1 & 2		In SUPPORT to FESTUBERT Sector	
"	3		Bn relieved by 1/5th Bn Kings Own R.L. Regt and after relief took over Right Subsector, GIVENCHY Sector from 1/4th Bn Kings Own - R.L. Regt	
"	4 to 8		Usual trench routine	
"	9		Relieved by 1/5th Lancs Fusiliers and moved to VAUDRICOURT	
VAUDRICOURT	10 to 14		Training	
"	15		Relieved 1/5th Bn South Lancs Regt in SUPPORT to FESTUBERT SECTOR	
Trenches	16 & 17		Usual routine and Working Parties	
"	18		Relieved 1/6th K.L.R. in Left Subsector, FESTUBERT Sector	
"	20		Relieved by 1/5th South Lancs Regt and then took over the Left Subsector, GIVENCHY Sector	
"	23		Relieved by units of 164 Inf Bde and moved to VAUDRICOURT	
VAUDRICOURT	24 to 26		Training	
"	27		Relieved 2/5th Lancs Fusiliers on Left subsector, GIVENCHY SECTOR	
Trenches	30		Relieved by 1/6th K.L.R. and moved into SUPPORT	

O H Potter Lieut. Col
Comdg 1/4th Bn "The Kings" (Liverpool Regt) J.S.

WAR DIARY or INTELLIGENCE SUMMARY

Army Form C. 2118.

(Erase heading not required.)

Instructions regarding War Diaries and Intelligence Summaries are contained in F.S. Regs., Part II. and the Staff Manual respectively. Title pages will be prepared in manuscript.

Place	Date	Hour	Summary of Events and Information	Remarks and references to Appendices
Vieille Chapelle	August 1918 1 & 2		In Support to FESTUBERT Sector	
"	3		Bn relieved by 1/5th Bn Kings Own R.L.Regt and after relief took over Right Subsector, GIVENCHY Sector from 1/4th Bn Kings Own R.L.Regt	
"	4 to 8		Usual trench routine	
"	9		Relieved by 1/5th Lanc Fusiliers and moved to VAUDRICOURT	
VAUDRICOURT	10 to 14		Training	
"	15		Relieved 1/5th Bn South Lanc Regt in Support to FESTUBERT Sector	
Gorre	16 & 17		Usual routine and Working Parties	
"	18		Relieved 1/6th K.L.R. in L/S Subsector, FESTUBERT Sector	
"	20		Relieved by 1/5th South Lancs Regt and then took over the Left Subsector, GIVENCHY Sector	
"	23		Relieved by units of 164 Inf Bde and moved to VAUDRICOURT	
VAUDRICOURT	24 to 26		Training	
"	27		Relieved 2/5th Lanc Fusiliers in Left Subsector, GIVENCHY Sector	
Gorre	30		Relieved by 1/6th K.L.R. and moved into Support	

Comdg. 1/4th Bn "The King's" (Spec. Regt) S.S. Lieut. Col.

Secret & Confidential.

War Diary
for the month of
September 1918.

1/4th Bn. "The King's" (Liverpool Regt)

165/55
9R 4 3

39e

War Diary
of
11th Liverpool R
for period
1st to 30th Septr
1918

Army Form C. 2118.

1/4th Bn The Kings (Spool Regiment) SS

WAR DIARY
or
INTELLIGENCE SUMMARY.

(Erase heading not required.)

Instructions regarding War Diaries and Intelligence Summaries are contained in F. S. Regs., Part II. and the Staff Manual respectively. Title pages will be prepared in manuscript.

Place	Date Sept 1918	Hour	Summary of Events and Information	Remarks and references to Appendices
TRENCHES	1		In Support Sector, Right Brigade. Usual Routine.	
— " —	2		Relieved by 1/4th Bn Kings Own R.L. Regt and took over Right Subsector, by Left Brigade from 1/10th (Scottish) Bn K.L.R.	
— " —	3		Enemy withdrawal commenced.	
— " —	4 & 5		Line advanced to CHAPELLE ST ROCH and VIOLANES TRENCH	
— " —	8		Relieved by 1/10th (Scottish) Bn K.L.R. and moved to DROUVIN CAMP	
DROUVIN CAMP	9 to 14		Training	
Trenches	14		Relieved 1/4th K.L.S. Regt. in Right Support Sector, Right Brigade.	
"	18.		At B Coys at disposal O/C 1/5th Kings for Operation on CANTELEUX TRENCH and APSE HOUSE — Successful. Relieved 1/5th Kings in Outpost Line.	
Outpost line	20		In conjunction with operation advanced by Left Bde on Left mounting STRONG FARM BELT, BUTTON over BRACES TRENCHES VIOLANES X roads and VIOLANES CHATEAU occupied and Relieved by 1/4th Bn Kings Own R.L. Regt and moved to VAUDRICOURT CAMP	
VAUDRICOURT CAMP	21 & 22		Training	
Trenches	23		Relieved 1/5th B.L. Regt in Reserve — LEFT BRIGADE	
"	25		Relieved 1/5th St L Regt in Support — do —	
"	27		Relieved — do — in Outpost — do —	
"	29		Operation in occupying PIANOHOUSE (see att. a/c and narrative) Relieved by 1/5th Bn Kings Own R L Regt and moved into billets	
BETHUNE	30		in BETHUNE	

1/7th Bn "The Kings" (Lpool Regt) S.S.

Narrative of Events, 29.9.18.

On the morning of 29th September 1918, 4 Platoons were ordered to attack enemy positions on the LA BASSEE ROAD, S.W. of LORGIES, objectives being from S.30.c.95.65 to S.30.a.70.70, to be supported by Artillery and S.M's. One Platoon was ordered to deliver a secondary attack on houses in the eastern outskirts of VIOLANES, this attack being without Artillery preparation.

For the attack on the LA BASSEE ROAD assembly positions were taken up with the right flank at S.30.c.45.55 and the left flank in SAUCY TRENCH S.30.a.25.60. A slight enemy barrage was put down whilst these platoons were waiting for ZERO. The platoon attacking in VIOLANES and took up a position along road at A.6.a.15.60.

At ZERO 4.55 am the Platoons advanced and reached their objectives. No. 16 Platoon supported by No. 15 Platoon found the house at S.30.c.95.60 strongly held. 4 Prisoners were taken and 2 of the enemy killed, but after a hard fight these Platoons were unable to capture the positions and withdrew having had 9 casualties including an officer. No. 14 Platoon reached their objectives and found no enemy. No. 13 Platoon reached the dugouts in S.30.a.70.70. which they found strongly held. They were unable to capture same and withdrew having 4 casualties and inflicting casualties on the enemy. No. 3 Platoon in VIOLANES took both their objectives capturing 2 M.G's and 4 prisoners and inflicted casualties. They established themselves in the captured positions

Meantime the enemy barrage had increased to great intensity on PIANO HOUSE and SAUCY TRENCH and the enemy launched an attack at 5.40 am on this area, which was being held by Nos. 7 & 8 Platoons. With the exception of 1 Officer and 3 Other Ranks Wounded only 1 Sgt and 6 Other Ranks got away.

2/Lieut. STOTT and his platoon holding house in VIOLANES saw the enemy advancing on dugout S.30.c.10.30. during this attack and by prompt bringing the captured M.G's into use, he broke up this part of the attack.

At 3 pm a counter-attack was launched the objectives being the ground lost in the morning, also to occupy houses at S.29.b.90.50. The attack was carried out by one Platoon A Coy under 2/Lt. RILEY, one Platoon D Coy under 2/Lt. STEPHENS and ½ Platoon D Coy under 2/Lieut. JOEL, the latter platoon to occupy the house in S.29.b.90.50. The assembly position of these Platoons was SAUCY TRENCH.

One Platoon of 'C' Coy under 2/Lieut. KENSHOLE supported by ½ Platoon D Coy were detailed to attack the junction of SPARTAN TRENCH and LA BASSEE ROAD and if this was not held to move on to the dugouts in STRASBURG TRENCH.

The attack was made under an intense barrage of 18 pdrs. and was successful, all objectives being taken.

2/Lieut. KENSHOLE pursued the enemy up STRASBURG TRENCH and succeeded in forcing his well past the concrete dugouts, capturing a

M.G. A block was made in the trench about S.24.c.99.10. which was held in spite of repeated attacks.

On completion of the operation the 2 Platoons of A & D Coys withdrew and 2/Lieut. KENSHOLE and his platoon supported by ½ Platoon of D Coy held the positions until relieved by the 1/5th Bn "King's Own" R.L. Regt. at 3 am morning 30th September 1918.

2nd October 1918.

C.K. Potter
Lt. Col.
COMDG 7TH BN THE KING'S (L'POOL.) REGT

S E C R E T.

OPERATION ORDERS No. 81,
BY LIEUT.COL.C.K.POTTER, D.S.O., M.C.,
Comdg.1/7th Bn. "The King's" (L'pool Regiment) T.F.

In the Field.   28.9.18.   Saturday.

Copy No......

Reference Map:- RUE DU MARAIS, 1/10,000.

1. INTENTION. 1/7th K.L.R. will attack LA BASSEE ROAD from S.30.d.05.60 to S.30.a.60.70, including group of dugouts at S.30.a.70.70 and secure prisoners. A secondary attack will be made on houses in VIOLAINES A.6.a.45.45. and A.6.a.35.15.

2. OBJECTIVES.
   No.16 Platoon - Concrete dugout and road junction S.30.c.95.65.
   No.15 Platoon - Will support No.16 Platoon and on capture of objectives will occupy dugout and push forward patrol into BEAU PUITS at ZERO plus 15.
   No.14 Platoon - LA BASSEE ROAD from S.30.c.90.95 to S.30.a.65.40
   No.13 Platoon - Group of dugouts S.30.a.70.70.
   One Platoon of "A" Coy (2/Lt.STOTT) will attack house A.6.a.45.45.

   On capture of concrete dugout No.16 Platoon will move along LA BASSEE ROAD to road junction S.30.d.20.25, thence along road to point A.6.a.45.40, where they will join up with the Platoon of "A" Company and will attack and capture house A.6.a.35.15. These two posts will be subsequently occupied by 2/Lt. STOTT'S Platoon.

   On completion of operations Nos.16, 14 and 13 Platoons will withdraw to Support Company positions.

   The Platoon of "B" Coy holding PIANO HOUSE will co-operate from flank and will push up STRASBURG TRENCH at ZERO plus 4 and occupy concrete dugouts S.24.c.85.05.

3. ASSEMBLY POSITIONS. O.C. "D" Company will arrange for assembly positions as follows:-
   No.16 Platoon - Right flank at S.30.c.45.55 to point about S.30.d.40.85.
   No.15 Platoon - Will form up in rear of No.16 Platoon.
   No.14 Platoon - From left of No.16 Platoon S.30.d.40.85, to point about S.30.a.25.30.
   No.13 Platoon - SAUCY TRENCH about S.30.a.28.40. to S.30.a.25.60.
   The Platoon of "A" Coy will form up along N.E.side of road about A.6.a.15.60.

4. FORWARD REPORT CENTRE will be established by Lieut.MARWOOD at "B" Coy.Hqrs. S.29.d.30.70, 1 hour before ZERO.

5. PRISONERS will be taken to "B" Coy.Hqrs. O.C. "B" Coy will arrange for necessary escort to Bn.Hqrs.

6. DUMPS. Dumps of S.A.A. and Bombs have been formed at road junction S.29.d.40.60 and at point S.29.b.02.35.

7. MEDICAL. Forward Dressing Station will be established at S.29.b.10.35. S.B.Relay Post will be established on road S.29.a.30.52 by O.C. "B" Coy, who will send his reserve S.B's; also reserve S.B's of "A" Company.

8. SYNCHRONIZATION. Watches will be synchronised at "D" Coys. present Hqrs at 8 p.m. and 12 midnight.

9. DRESS. Light Fighting Order for Nos.13, 14 and 16 Platoons, i.e. without haversacks. No.15 Platoon and Platoon "A" Coy - Battle Order.

10. ZERO HOUR will be at 4.55 a.m. 29th September 1918, at which hour all troops will attack. Attacking Troops will be in assembly positions ½ hour before ZERO.

- 2 -

11. ARTILLERY, MACHINE GUN, and TRENCH MORTAR PROGRAMME attached.

These orders have been communicated verbally to officers concerned.

ACKNOWLEDGE.

[signature] Captain,
Adjt.1/7th Bn."The King's" (Liverpool Regiment) T.F.

28th September 1918.

ARTILLERY, MACHINE GUN, and TRENCH MORTAR PROGRAMME.

ARTILLERY.

Three (possibly six) batteries 18 pdrs. will open on LA BASSEE ROAD from S.30.d.10.45 to S.30.a.65.45 at ZERO.

At ZERO plus 2 barrage will be lifted to road from about S.30.d.75.95 to S.30.a.98.60 to ZERO plus 15, when it will die away.

The Right Battery will move sideways along LA BASSEE ROAD from ZERO Plus 2 and will remain on road south of point S.30.d.20.25 to ZERO plus 10.
At ZERO plus 10 it will fire on LA BASSEE TRENCH astride LA BASSEE ROAD until ZERO plus 15.

4.5 Hows. will fire on BEAU PUITS from ZERO to ZERO plus 15.

MACHINE GUNS will also co-operate.

TRENCH MORTARS.

2 Stokes Mortars will fire on group of dugouts S.30.a.70.65 from ZERO to ZERO plus 2.
At ZERO plus 2 they will lift to STRASBURG TRENCH about S.24.d.45.30 to Zero plus 4.

1 Stokes Mortar in addition will be firing on this point from Zero to Zero plus 4, when they will all cease.

[signature] Captain,
Adjt.1/7th Bn. "The King's" (Liverpool Regiment) T.F.

28th September 1918.

SECRET & CONFIDENTIAL

War Diary

for the month of

October 1918.

1/4th Bn "The Kings" (Lpool Regt).

Army Form C. 2118.

WAR DIARY
or
INTELLIGENCE SUMMARY.
(Erase heading not required.)

Instructions regarding War Diaries and Intelligence Summaries are contained in F.S. Regs., Part II. and the Staff Manual respectively. Title pages will be prepared in manuscript.

Place	Date	Hour	Summary of Events and Information	Remarks and references to Appendices
BETHUNE	1-X-18	09.00 12.30	Companies Training under Company Commanders. 14.00-16.00 GAMES.	
	2-X-18	09.00 to 12.30	do 14.00-16.00 GAMES.	
BETHUNE	3-X-18	07.00	Battalion moved up in Motor lorries to 'SCURRY' positions. Battn Hd. Qrs. at BATTERSEA BRIDGE. Companies holding Canal Bridge head defences.- Advance commenced.	
LE PREOL	4-X-18		Companies holding Canal Bridge head defences.	
LE PREOL	5-X-18	09.00	Battalion marched to SALOME in support to the Outpost Battalion.	
SALOME	6-X-18		Companies employed on making main line of resistance etc.	
SALOME	7-X-18		do . Battalion moved to HANTAY	
HANTAY			and took over the Outpost line from the 6th K.L.R.	
- do -	8-X-18		Outpost Battalion	
HANTAY	9-X-18		Outpost Battalion	
Grand Moisnil	10-X-18		Outpost Battalion. So de-stuffed on to new Divisional frontage. 'A' Coy PETIT HANTAY. 'B' Coy HANTAY, 'C' Coy LA BOURSE, 'D' Coy HOCRON - BASSÉ RUE AREA. Battalion were relieved in the Outpost line by the 5th 12th K.L.R. and went into Billets in LA BASSÉE an BRIGADE RESERVE	
LA BASSÉE	11-X-18		Companies Bathing and Cleaning up	
	12-X-18	09.00 to 12.30	Companies Training under Company Commanders.	
- do -	13-X-18	- do -	do	
- do -	14-X-18	- do -	do	
- do -	15-X-18	- do -	do	
LA BASSÉE (Grand Moisnil)	16-X-18		Battalion moved up to GRAND MOISNIL - LA PLACE AREA in Reserve to Brigade.	
HOCRON SECLIN	17-X-18	06.30	Battalion Hd. Qrs moved to HOCRON and at 13.30 marched via DON - ANNOEULON - ALLENES - GONDECOURT to SECLIN, where it billeted for the night. Advance continued	

Army Form C. 2118.

WAR DIARY
or
INTELLIGENCE SUMMARY.

(Erase heading not required.)

Place	Date	Hour	Summary of Events and Information	Remarks and references to Appendices
SECLIN. FRETIN	18.X.18	08.00	The Battalion became Advanced Guard Battalion and passed through the Outpost line at 08.00. 1 Battery 18 pdrs + 2 4.5" How's, 4 Sec M.G.C. - 1 Sec Field Coy R.E. and Specialist Rifles were attached to the Battalion for this purpose. The first objective, the high ground in front of GRAND ENNETIERES was reached without opposition at 09.00 and patrols pushed forward to FRETIN. ST VAAST FARM was occupied at 09.30 and FRETIN was cleared and entered at 10.25 and patrols were pushed forward onto HUVET and posts established covering Bridgeheads over LEMARCQ RIVER, which were held by the enemy. ENNEVELIN was reached without opposition and patrols pushed forward to HELIN and LARIN 10.30. All objectives were gained by 12.45. LA BRUSZ FME and the LAUNDRY East of LEMARCQ RIVER were captured and outposts were established for the Night holding all Bridge heads with forward posts. Battalion Hd Qrs were established in FRETIN.	
FRETIN CYSOING	19.X.18		The Battalion continued as Advance Guard at 09.00. LE MARCQ RIVER was crossed at 09.00. LOUVIL was occupied at 09.35 and patrols sent forward to STATION at CYSOING and QUENNAMONT. CYSOING and QUENNAMONT were entered when cleared and patrols went forward through Bois de CYSOING on to BOURGHELLES and BACHY. These places being occupied patrols pushed on to ESPLECHIN and SANTIERE. Outpost picquet line for the night was established East of Bois de FOUGERE and BACHY. Batt H.Q. at CYSOING.	
CYSOING FROIDMONT	20.X.18		The Battalion continued as advanced Guard and passed through the Picquet line at 09.00 and advanced on FROIDMONT through MARAICHE and ESPLECHIN. Opposition was encountered in FROIDMONT CHATEAU WOOD. FROIDMONT being cleared Companies pushed forward through HILLEMEAU and MARNIERE where strong opposition was encountered. Outpost picquet line was established for the night along Eastern outskirts of HILLEMEAU with posts forward. The Battalion was relieved at 20.00 by the 5th K.L.R. Coys billeting in HILLEMEAU - FROIDMONT - ESPLECHIN AREA.	

Army Form C. 2118.

WAR DIARY
or
INTELLIGENCE SUMMARY.

(Erase heading not required.)

Instructions regarding War Diaries and Intelligence Summaries are contained in F. S. Regs., Part II. and the Staff Manual respectively. Title pages will be prepared in manuscript.

Place	Date	Hour	Summary of Events and Information	Remarks and references to Appendices
FROIDMONT WANNEHAIN	21.X.18	14.00	Battalion was relieved by the 10th K.L.R and marched to rest billets at WANNEHAIN.	
— do —	22.X.18		Baths and cleaning up.	
— do —	23.X.18	09.00 12.30	Companies Training under Company Commanders.	
— do —	24.X.18	09.00 12.30	do	
— do —	25.X.18	09.00 12.30	do	
— do —	26.X.18	09.00 12.30	do	
— do —	27.X.18		CHURCH PARADE	
— do —	28.X.18		Battalion moved to MAIN LINE of RESISTANCE. Battalion Hd Qrs. FARM du BARON.	
ESPLECHIN	29.X.18		MAIN LINE of RESISTANCE.	
— do —	30.X.18		MAIN LINE of RESISTANCE. Battalion moved to Outpost Line FROIDMONT-ÈRE	
FROIDMONT	31.X.18		OUTPOST LINE.	
— do —				

Lt Col.
COMDG 7TH BN THE KING'S (L'POOL) REGT

165/55 98/45

War Diary
of
17th Howitzer R
for period
1st to 30th Nov
1918

41e

Army Form C. 2118.

WAR DIARY
of
INTELLIGENCE SUMMARY.
(Erase heading not required.)

Instructions regarding War Diaries and Intelligence Summaries are contained in F. S. Regs., Part II. and the Staff Manual respectively. Title pages will be prepared in manuscript.

Place	Date Nov 1918	Hour	Summary of Events and Information	Remarks and references to Appendices
W. of TOURNAI	1.		Outpost Battalion	
- do -	2.		Raid on WOOD West of TOURNAI, carried out by "C" Coy, resulted in capture of 8 prisoners and 2 Moltene Guns, 15 enemy being killed. Our casualties 6 Other Ranks wounded.	
- do -	3.		Relieved in Outpost Line by 1/5th Kings and moved into Bde Reserve in billets in FROIDMONT.	
FROIDMONT	4 to 6		Baths, Training and Inspections by Coy & Bomb Officers.	
- do -	7.		Relieved 1/6th Kings on "Main Line of Resistance".	
Frs. DU BARON	8.		German withdrawal commenced. 1/6th Kings occupied TOURNAI up to West bank of River ESCAUT during day. Bn. moved up to billets in Eastern portion FROIDMONT.	
FROIDMONT	9.		River ESCAUT bridged in early morning and Advanced Guard 1/6th Kings and 1/6th Kings occupied FROIDNANTEAU and BECLERS, were joined with little opposition. 1 O.R. wounded.	
-	10.		STOCKNEM'S FORCE passed through. Bn. marched to GRANDMETZ where 2 Companies and Bn. HQrs rested for the night. Two Companies continued on to LIGNÉ and took up Outpost positions.	
-	11.		165 Inf Bde assembled at LIGNÉ to continue the advance. Shortly after 10.00 hours it was announced that an armistice had been signed and that hostilities would cease at 11.00 hours. After 11.00 hours the Bn. moved off to billets in LANQUESAINT.	
LANQUESAINT	12 to 16.		Training and recreation. Working party on Railway Reconstruction.	
- do -	17.		- do - Voluntary Church Services	
- do -	18.		- do -	
- do -	19.		Played Route. 1st Kings. Great Match. Bde. Football Competition. 3rd Fld Amb. 0.	
- do -	20-22		Route. 1st Kings 7 - 7/1st W.S.	
- do -	23.		Training and Recreation Route Football Match. 7th Kings 2. 6th Kings 0.	
- do -	24.		Church Parade Services and inspections of Feet.	

Army Form C. 2118.

WAR DIARY
or
INTELLIGENCE SUMMARY.

(Erase heading not required.)

Instructions regarding War Diaries and Intelligence Summaries are contained in F. S. Regs., Part II. and the Staff Manual respectively. Title pages will be prepared in manuscript.

Place	Date Nov 1918	Hour	Summary of Events and Information	Remarks and references to Appendices
LANQUESAINT	25	-	Bathing - Inter-platoon football matches (first Round)	
- do -	26	-	Training and Recreation. Bn football team defeated 5th Kings team by 5 goals to Nil.	
- do -	27	-	Training and Recreation.	
- do -	28	-	do 2nd Round of Inter-Platoon Competition.	
- do -	29	-	do Bn team 10 goals - 165 Bde team 0 goals.	
- do -	30	-	Bn Cross Country Run for all ranks.	

Lt Col.
COMDG 7TH BN THE KING'S (L'POOL) REGT

90146

42e.

War Diary
of
11th Liverpool R
for period
1st to 31st December
1918.

Army Form C. 2118.

WAR DIARY
INTELLIGENCE SUMMARY.
(Erase heading not required.)

Instructions regarding War Diaries and Intelligence Summaries are contained in F.S. Regs., Part II. and the Staff Manual respectively. Title pages will be prepared in manuscript.

Place	Date 1918	Hour	Summary of Events and Information	Remarks and references to Appendices
ARQUEBRINT	Dec. 1		Church Parades	
"	2		Baths + Education	
"	3		Training + Education	
"	4		Battalion Drill and route march	
"	5-6		Training + Education	
"	7		Visit to Division by His Majesty the King on main ATH - TOURNAI ROAD.	
"	8		Church Parades	
"	9+10		Training + Education	
"	11		Route March	
"	12		Baths. Lectures by M.O. + Education	
"	13		Training and Education	
"	14		Cleaning up and repairing billets	
"	15		March to Brussels area and commenced at 1125 hrs. Arrived ENGHIEN at 1600 hrs.	
ENGHIEN	16		Left at 0900 hrs and arrived BUYSINGHEM 1830 hrs	
BUYSINGHEM	17		Left at 0900 hrs and arrived UCCLE about 1200 hrs.	
UCCLE	18		Inspections	
"	19		Baths	
"	20+21		Training and Education	
"	22		Church Parades	
"	23		Route March	
"	24		Training and Education	
"	25		Church Parade. Bn. Christmas Dinner and Festivities	
"	26		Route March	
"	27		Training and Education	
"	28		Church Parades	
"	29		Baths and Education	
"	30		Training and Education	
"	31			

O.R.P.M. Lt Col.
COMDG 1/7TH BN THE KING'S (L'POOL) REGT

9847

43e

War Diary
of
11" Liverpool K
for review
1st to 31st January
1919

Army Form C. 2118.

WAR DIARY
INTELLIGENCE SUMMARY.
(Erase heading not required.)

Instructions regarding War Diaries and Intelligence Summaries are contained in F.S. Regs., Part II. and the Staff Manual respectively. Title pages will be prepared in manuscript.

Place	Date	Hour	Summary of Events and Information	Remarks and references to Appendices
UCCLE	Sep. 1919			
	1		Training	
	2		Inspection by Commdg Officer and Training	
	3		King of Belgians attended March past of Division on occasion 2nd anniversary of formation	
	4		Training and Education	
	5		Church Parades	
	6 to 9		Training and Education	
	10		Route March	
	11		Baths. Div. Cross-country run	
	12		Church Parades	
	13		Inspection by Commdg Offr	
	14		Route March	
	15		Training and Education	
	16		do do Semi-final Div. Football Competition. Result 7th Kings 3, 7/5 L.F.s 2	
	17		do do 1st day Div. Boxing Tournament	
	18		do do 2nd do do	
	19		Church Parades	
	20		Training and Education 3rd do do	
	21		Route March	
	22 to 24		Training and Education	
	25		Baths	
	26		Review of III Corps troops by King of Belgians in Brussels	
	27		Training and Education Result 7th Kings 4, 166 Bde Sigs 2	
	28		do Final Div. Football Competition.	
	29		do	
	30 to 31		Training	

Comdg 1/7th Bn THE KING'S (L'POOL) REGT
Lt. Col.

WAR DIARY 1916

14th LIVERPOOL R

FEBRUARY 1917

44e

A.F.C. 2118

1/7TH L'POOL REGT
War Diary

Summary of Events and Information

Place	Date		
Uccle, Brussels, Belgium	FEB 1919		
	1.	Training & Parades	13 men proceeded for Demobilization
	2.	Church	1 Offr. & 9 " " " Demobilization
	3.	Baths	4 men proceeded for Demobilization
	4.	Training and Education	Lecture on V.D.
	5.	Training and Education	Lecture by C.O. on Army of Occupation.
	6.	Training and Education	5 men proceeded for Demobilization
	7.	Training and Kit inspections	6 men proceeded for demobilization
	8.	Church and Education	Lecture by C.O. on Army of Occupation – 11 men pro. for demob.
	9.	Parades and Education	6 " " " demobilization. also 1 Offr. (Lt. Bolton)
	10.	Training	
	11.	Training	
	12.	Baths	
	13.	Re-organisation of Battalion – 6 men proceeded for demobilization
	14.	Standing in Lines and inspections of kit – 11 men proceeded for demobilization
	15.	do	17 do
	16.	Church Parades	18 do
	17.	Training, Education and inspections	21 do
	18.	Training and Education	
	19.	Training and Education	
	20.	Baths	
	21.	Training and Education	7 do
	22.	Training – Lecture on Battle of Waterloo by Senior Chaplain – 34 do
	23.	Church Parades	20 do
	24.	Training – Visit to Waterloo of men who attended lecture – 25 do
	25.	Training and Inspections	
	26.	Training	21 do
	27.	Training	
	28.	Baths	

C.Ritter
Lt.Col.
COMDG 7TH Bn. THE KING'S (L'POOL REGT)

WAR DIARY No 49

1/4th LIVERPOOL R

MARCH 1917

45¢

Army Form C. 2118.

WAR DIARY
or
INTELLIGENCE SUMMARY.
(Erase heading not required.)

Instructions regarding War Diaries and Intelligence Summaries are contained in F. S. Regs., Part II. and the Staff Manual respectively. Title pages will be prepared in manuscript.

Place	Date	Hour	Summary of Events and Information	Remarks and references to Appendices
Brussels	1919 March 1		Training	
	2		Church Parades	
	3		Training and Education	
	4		Training	
	5		Training and Education	
	6		Training	
	7		Draft of 7 Offrs and 170 O.R. proceeded to join 4th K.R.R. reducing Battalion to Cadre Strength	
Uccle	8 to 31		Checking and sorting stores and equipment.	

[signature]
Lt Col
COMDG 7TH BN THE KING'S (L'POOL) REGT

Vol 50

46.e

Secret & Confidential

War Diary
for the month of
April 1919.

1/1st Bn "The King's" (Lpool Regt)

WAR DIARY
or
INTELLIGENCE SUMMARY.
(Erase heading not required.)

Army Form C. 2118.

Place	Date	Hour	Summary of Events and Information	Remarks references to Appendices
Nord, Brussels	1/30.4.19		Drawn to Extra Establishment awaiting to be transferred to Engineers	

J.R. Hewton ← Lt Col
COMDG. 1st Bn THE KING'S (L'POOL) REGT

www.ingramcontent.com/pod-product-compliance
Lightning Source LLC
Chambersburg PA
CBHW081412160426
43193CB00013B/2160